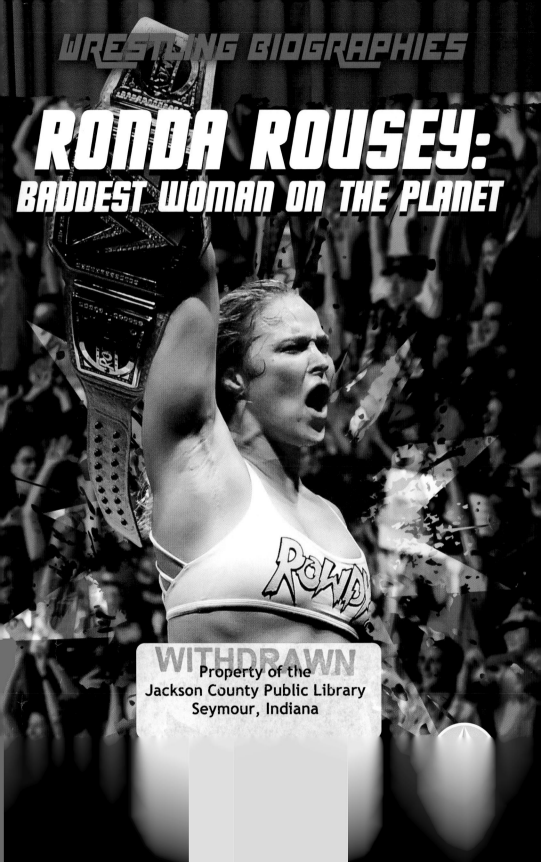

RONDA ROUSEY:
BADDEST WOMAN ON THE PLANET

abdobooks.com

Published by Abdo Zoom, a division of ABDO, P.O. Box 398166, Minneapolis,
Minnesota 55439. Copyright © 2020 by Abdo Consulting Group, Inc. International
copyrights reserved in all countries. No part of this book may be reproduced in any
form without written permission from the publisher. Fly!™ is a trademark and logo
of Abdo Zoom.

Printed in the United States of America, North Mankato, Minnesota.
052019
092019

Photo Credits: Alamy, AP Images, Redux Pictures, Seth Poppel/Yearbook Library,
Shutterstock, © Miguel Discart p10 / CC BY-SA 2.0
Production Contributors: Kenny Abdo, Jennie Forsberg, Grace Hansen
Design Contributors: Dorothy Toth, Neil Klinepier

Library of Congress Control Number: 2018963796

Publisher's Cataloging-in-Publication Data

Names: Abdo, Kenny, author.
Title: Ronda Rousey: baddest woman on the planet / by Kenny Abdo.
Other title: Baddest woman on the planet
Description: Minneapolis, Minnesota : Abdo Zoom, 2020 | Series: Wrestling
    biographies set 2 | Includes online resources and index.
Identifiers: ISBN 9781532127540 (lib. bdg.) | ISBN 9781532128523 (ebook) |
    ISBN 9781532129018 (Read-to-me ebook)
Subjects: LCSH: Rousey, Ronda--Juvenile literature. | Wrestlers--United States--
    Biography--Juvenile literature. | World Wrestling Entertainment Studios--
    Juvenile literature.
Classification: DDC 796.812092 [B]--dc23

TABLE OF CONTENTS

RONDA
ROUSEY

4

From the rings of the UFC to the WWE, Rowdy Ronda Rousey has fought to rule them all! Rousey has built a mountain of **championship** wins, titles, and records. And she has no plans to stop anytime soon.

EARLY YEARS

Ronda Jean Rousey was born in
Riverside, California, in 1987.

She competed in Women's Judo during the 2004 Olympic games at 17. At her next Olympic games appearance in 2008, Rousey won the Bronze medal.

Rousey was the first woman to sign up for UFC in 2012. She was the first and longest leading **Bantamweight** champion for more than two years.

Rousey's first WWE appearance was at the end of WrestleMania 31. The Rock was mad at the Authority, a team made up of Stephanie McMahon and Triple-H. He spotted Rousey in the audience and asked for her help. She assisted the Rock in tossing the Authority from the ring.

11

In 2017, Rousey signed a full-time contract with WWE. She took the nickname "Rowdy" from her friend Roddy Piper. He gave her full permission to carry on the name.

At WrestleMania 34, Rousey
was teamed up with Kurt Angle
against the Authority. Rousey
submitted Stephanie McMahon,
winning the match.

Rousey fought Alexa Bliss during **SummerSlam** in 2018. She defeated Bliss to take home the Women's **Championship**!

Outside of the ring, Rousey is a **bona fide** movie star. She has been in blockbuster hits like *Furious 7, The Expendables 3,* and *Mile 22.*

18

Rousey was inducted into the UFC **Hall of Fame** in 2018. She is the first female to receive the honor. Rousey was inducted into the International Sports Hall of Fame the same year.

GLOSSARY

Bantamweight – a weight class in fighting sports between 112 lbs (51 kg) and 118 lbs (54 kg).

bona fide – real and legitimate.

championship – a game, match, or race held to find a first-place winner.

debut – to appear for the first time.

Hall of Fame – an award given to an individual for a lifetime of work.

submit – when a wrestler is able to make their opponent give up.

SummerSlam – a major WWE show held every year in August.

ONLINE RESOURCES

Booklinks
NONFICTION NETWORK
FREE! ONLINE NONFICTION RESOURCES

To learn more about Ronda Rousey, please visit **abdobooklinks.com** or scan this QR code. These links are routinely monitored and updated to provide the most current information available.

INDEX

CPSIA information can be obtained at www.ICGtesting.com
Printed in the USA
BVOW03*1537091014

370198BV00012B/88/P

ABOUT THE AUTHOR

Ernest A. Gallo

Graduate of Philadelphia Wireless Technical Institute with undergraduate studies at the University of Maryland.

While serving in the Navy Reserve, left active duty as a Second Class Petty Officer—Communications Technician, Maintenance Branch (CTM-2).

USS *Liberty* Survivor

Completed a 27.5 year career with the Central Intelligence Agency and received the CIA's civilian intelligence award, the CIA Commendation Medal.

Following the CIA, worked for GTE, Quality Services Incorporated, TriCorps, Marconi International and British Aerospace Enterprises (BAE) taking him into retirement.

Ernie is a member of: the Elks; Veterans of Foreign Wars; The Navy League of the United States, Naval Cryptologic Veterans Association; the USS Liberty Veterans Association, and the American Cold War Veterans. He is the current and former President and Vice President of the USS Liberty Veterans Association and founder of the Liberty Foundation.

References

Books:

- *A Republic, Not an Empire*; author, Patrick Buchanan
- *Assault on The Liberty*; author, James Ennes, Jr
- *Beyond Treason Reflections on the Cover-up of the June 1967 Israeli Attack on the USS Liberty an American Spy Ship*; author, Robert J. Allen, JD
- *Body of Secrets*; author, James Bamford
- *Guilt by Association*, author, Jeff Gates
- *Operation Cyanide*, author, Peter Hounan
- *Palestine, Peace Not Apartheid*, author, Jimmy Carter
- *The Attack on the Liberty*, author, James Scott
- *The High Cost of Peace*, author, Yossef Bodansky
- *The Liberty Cipher & Deception*; author, Patrick Pacalo, PHD
- *What I Saw That Day*, author Phil Tourney
- *Woman from Mossad*, author, Peter Hounan

Films:

- *Dead in the Water*; BBC Films
- *Justice for the Liberty*, Break of Dawn Production
- History Undercover, Cover Up: Attack on the USS Liberty, the History Channel

Web Sites:

- www.ussliberty.org or www.usslibertyveterans.org
- www.usslibertyinquiry.com
- http://home.cfl.rr.com/gidusko/liberty

Chapter 1

America Changed Since 1967

What happened?

A devastating event occurred in my life compelling me to write this book. It is very difficult for me to find the words to explain how much it forever changed my life and my way of thinking. To wit: The USS Liberty was ordered to an intercept location off the Sinai coast by the Joint Chiefs in order to confirm Soviet and other Communist block countries non involvement in the Arab/Israeli war. That is, on June 8, 1967, without any warning, Israeli Defense Forces (IDF) deliberately, violently, and brutally attacked a United States Navy Intelligence ship, the USS Liberty AGTR-5, in international waters killing thirty-four Americans and wounding 174. Of the 174, some became maimed and their lives appreciatively shortened. One sailor, Larry Weaver, required thirty-four operations to maintain his current health. Most of the survivors, for reasons I will identify, suffer from PTSD. In my estimation, any other country that planned and executed an attack of this magnitude would require a military response from the United States. Obviously, that did not happen. Why?

As I will expound, the above event initiates the transition our wonderful country decided to take—a profound negative turn which affects all Americans and the Middle East. The road taken by the Johnson Administration in 1967 continues and is nurtured by Israeli support organizations. This grip on America resulted in a very dangerous situation and to this day causes America to loose face as we are no longer a nation of laws. That is, Israel continues to defy international law and the United States protects and defends her actions. Therefore, we lost our American values. We lost our vision. As I will point out, the result eventually places Israel over and above American citizens and military. If Israel had any concern they could attempt to deliberately sink an American Navy ship and get away with it, the USS *Liberty* attack would have never happened.

The Before

Presidents Eisenhower and Kennedy maintained a balanced Middle East Policy. When the Israelis invaded the Sinai in 1956 and took over the Suez Canal with the assistance of Britain and France, Eisenhower successfully pressured them through the UN and other diplomatic means to turn over the operation and control of the Canal back to the Egyptians. To this day, I can still remember President Eisenhower's TV broadcast explaining his concern to the American public since the co-perpetrators were our close friends – Britain and France. Nevertheless, Eisenhower meant business and was prepared to intervene.

President Kennedy became upset and suspicious about

the Israelis developing nuclear weapons. He was very concerned about nuclear proliferation in that area of the world and communicated his concern to Israel regarding their activities at Dimona, their nuclear laboratory. As identified in Peter Hounam's book, "The Woman from Mossad," Mordechai Vanunu, an Israeli convert to Christianity, who worked at the site, blew the whistle on the fact the Israelis were manufacturing nuclear weapons.

The After

With President Johnson, things changed. From that point on, a now nuclear armed Israel could do no wrong and we became their primary arms supplier. In January 1968, the arms embargo on Israel was lifted and the sale of American weapons began to flow. By 1971, Israel was buying $600 million American-made weapons a year. Two years later the purchases topped $3 billion. Almost overnight, the Israeli Defense Forces (IDF) became the largest buyer of US-made arms and aircraft.

Elucidation

Let me clear the air as much as possible so that you know I have no hidden agenda. I am a traditionalist. I firmly believe in mom, pop, and apple pie. I would like to think of myself as an American patriot, however, what you are about to learn regarding the behavior of our government left me in much heart felt pain. While I should feel anger, I don't—but, yes—very frustrated and concerned. I can hardly get through the Star Spangle Banner without tears building up

in my eyes and I cannot sing "God Bless America" whatsoever for fear of totally breaking down. As you will learn, it appears to the *Liberty* survivors, America abandoned the crew of the USS *Liberty* to be sacrificed to or for our Israeli relationship. Let me make this very clear for you to understand—my Navy, under orders from the White House, abandoned us under fire! If you have any doubt, please read on.

As you will discover, in order to protect Washington's relationship with Israel, laws were broken:

- *Israel: machine-gunning our life rafts—a War Crime (Geneva Convention)*

- *Israel: forcefully taking Jordanian and Syrian land*

- *President Johnson: recall of aircraft—code of Military Conduct—not coming to the aid of US military under fire*

- *President Johnson: falsification of the Navy Court of Inquiry (code of Military Conduct)—obstruction of justice at the highest level.*

I am a proud member of the USS *Liberty* Veterans Association (LVA) – a 501c(3) charitable organization. The LVA is dedicated to getting the truth told. I am a former LVA President and Vice-President. I must state, the LVA members are not Jewish bigots or white supremacists, because our distracters love to label us as such. I have been called a Jew-hater, Nazi, conspiracy theorist and white-supremacist. However, I lovingly worship a Jewish carpenter and I cherish

my relationship with my Jewish friends and acquaintances. Above all, I am an eye witness to this tragedy. Please note, the LVA has many Jewish friends who support our American cause. (Please see chapter 8.)

I plan to explain why the USS *Liberty* Story may be the key to alert America to current trends. I will tell you the details of the attack. I will tell you details of the deceit and cover-up that occurred to the crew and the American public. I will tell you about the resultant impact on the lives of the crew (Navy and Marine Veterans). I will also tell you of the American patriots I have the privilege of knowing. In conclusion, I will provide my view in what is needed to change this country's current course. Because of my love of country, I want to create change and I hope and pray it is in time.

As you will see, our focus is with our government—not Israel. In order to prove to you our government is as complicit by not obtaining the facts of June 8, 1967, I will need to identify Israeli Defense Force (IDF) misdeeds. With that cited, some become very angry or offended. I would love to say, "Deal with it" because these are the facts—please remember we are eye witnesses. I understand this might be the first time you will hear what I am about to tell you of IDF actions. It may be very hard to take. Nevertheless, these are the honest facts and I would appreciate your respect for my attempt to explain them. For those, whom I met, believe that, in no uncertain terms, Israel cannot do anything wrong, burn this book.

From this point on, keep in mind that the USS *Liberty* is

the most decorated Navy ship for a single action. The medals awarded include: one Medal of Honor (our Captain), two Navy Crosses, twelve Silver Stars, twenty-six Bronze Stars, 208 Purple Hearts, the Presidential Unit Citation, and more. Except for a recent Silver Star awarded in 2009, none of the citations mention the attackers were Israeli.

The crew of the USS *Liberty* did everything possible not to give up our ship and fought the only way we could by maintaining our vital engineering propulsion machinery, water tight integrity, and most of all help keep our wounded alive. With the decorations mentioned, we have been dishonored and chastised by the lies of Israel and our own government. The United States Government does not understand that by joining with the IDF lie, they make the LVA appear as Jewish bigots and frustrate our efforts to distance ourselves from Neo Nazi organization that use us thereby aiding the bigot label. Ignoring the fact that since Israel used a torpedo, it was the willful attempted murder of 294 Americans; and, the administration never pressed Israel for the perpetrators of the attack. The government: does not realize the embarrassment to the crew as we are considered the "bad guys" for speaking up; put the Israeli relationship over and above the crew of the USS *Liberty*; and, dishonors the crew and our lost shipmates by making us a politically correct item of the day.

Note: This book is not written because of pent up anger toward Israel. On the contrary, we want the truth told by our government. If they do not know the truth, then they will need to complete an honest, objective, and thorough

investigation and publish the results. Why is this so important to us? Anything less than the truth dishonors the deceased crew, their families, and the medals awarded. For example, the Annapolis Naval Academy honors graduates who are killed in action by placing their names on a memorial honor wall in Bancroft Hall. USS *Liberty* crew Lt. Commander Philip Armstrong and Lt. Stephen Toth were killed and denied that privilege because their deaths were considered accidental; that is how the Washington bureaucrats wanted to handle it. It took the intervention of a four star admiral, Admiral Thomas Moorer, chairman of the Joint Chiefs, to rectify the wrong. Their names currently appear on the wall.

I guess we are supposed to keep our mouths shut—after all, Israel is our ally. I suppose if no one was killed or wounded, we could possibly do that. However, the fact that thirty-four were murdered, we would be remiss as Americans if we did not speak out, otherwise our shipmates died for nothing. Can you imagine how we would feel if Israel attacked another US Navy ship or aircraft and we said nothing? Ironically, nothing we say matters even though we are eye witnesses to the events of the day. In military and Congressional circles, it became politically correct to distance oneself from supporting the *Liberty* crew. These are the rules we have been subjected to for over forty-five years and especially the last twenty-five for speaking out. With the above in mind, the PTSD that the crew is still suffering is a time bomb I pray never explodes. I plead with you to divorce yourself from thinking of us in a negative light and simply think about the facts I will present.

The Playing Field

At this time, the official US Government position is in concert with the Israeli explanation of the attack. They want you to believe that it was a case of mistaken identity. The IDF stated in formal channels they believed they were attacking an Egyptian horse carrier seagoing vessel. However, this ship is half the size of the *Liberty* and had not been to sea since 1947. They must think some of us are gullible—at least some in our government must be. Ironically, the Israelis apologized and paid reparations for death, injuries, and the ship. The Israeli explanation is just plain "hog wash" and our politicians accepted the lie without challenge. Since the apology and acts of repentance are based on deceit, the crew of the *Liberty* does not accept their convenient and politically necessary contrition.

I would not be here if it were not for my shipmates especially the Naval Officers, Chiefs, Electronic Technicians, Radiomen, Engineers, and Damage Control Technicians. Most of the crew suffers some form of PTSD and keep their anger bottled up inside and that scares the hell out of me. My hope is by writing this book they can feel somewhat comforted. With the above in mind, how many more years will we be ignored and vilified for wanting the truth told?

The torpedo attack, producing a massive forty by twenty-five foot torpedo hole in her side, should have caused the USS Liberty to sink by all naval accounts. Two-thirds of the crew were either killed or wounded. I thank the Lord; I was not one of them. Some of the crew

realizes we are called to tell this story for the sake of America because our country is threatened from within. I will explain in detail.

Because of the attack and the subsequent cover-up, the USS *Liberty* crew have become well informed Americans regarding the Middle East. I, myself am very well read on current events and Middle East history. We came to realize that our Middle East policy since the Johnson administration resulted in actions at home and abroad equating to the same despicable Soviet Union actions we observed perpetrated in the height of the cold war. You have been lied to and misinformed both from our government and our news media. When it comes to Israel, America lacks a free press—resulting in a controlled press. This is why most Europeans feel differently toward the Middle East situation—more on that later.

My shipmates and I are loyal Americans and we will not knowingly divulge classified information. However, I will identify what I know about the USS *Liberty* for reasons that will become self evident. I visited over forty-five countries and lived overseas for ten years working for the CIA. There is no doubt in my mind that the United States' form of government is the best there is. I took an oath, twice, to support and defend the Constitution of the United States against all enemies, foreign and domestic. I have never been advised to stand down on that oath. The passion still exists. Some of us believe the Lord wants us to tell this story at this time. If it means anything, there is no doubt in my mind; I have a calling because of current Middle East events in

which America is involved. **God gave his grace to inspire our founding fathers** to create the most humane form of government and for other countries to emulate. That America is now very threatened.

With Old Glory, our Constitution, and the crew of the USS *Liberty* as a mental back drop, please read on.

Chapter 2

The Attack

The National Security Agency (NSA) had cleared personnel in all three services identified as security groups. They all performed the same basic duties tailored to the related service. The Naval Security Group personnel were identified as Communications Technicians (CTs). Secrecy and clearances were an absolute necessity. CTs were never permitted to discuss their activities with anyone including the remainder of the ships crew. Their skills included electronic and cryptographic communications and repair, signal intercept specialists (some with Morse code skills), linguists, communicators, and yeomen.

The USS *Liberty*, AGTR-5, was controlled primarily by the NSA. The ship, a converted WWII Victory hull cargo vessel, was one of the most advanced intelligence ships of the line. The USS *Liberty* had traditional American markings on her bow and stern (GTR 5) and across her stern (USS *LIBERTY*) and typically flew a five by eight foot American Flag from her center yardarm (flag pole). Our capabilities included radio, radar, and telemetry intercept. There were close to 150 security group personnel on board. Our mission was to intercept anything and everything in the ambient

ether normally around the west coast of Africa. The CT intercept area within the ship was approximately amid ship (the center), below the main deck, and in an enclosed and a denied area to the remainder of the crew. The area was sealed except for a single one door entrance (with a cipher number keyboard to enter) and an emergency escape hatch. This fact saved the ship from sinking.

The Attack

We departed from Norfolk, VA, for our planned four month cruise on May 2, 1967, arriving in Abidjan, Ivory Coast, Africa, on May 23rd. However, on May 24th, we were directed by the Joint Chiefs to immediately way anchor and proceed to Rota, Spain, at best possible speed. It took a good eight days of sailing arriving on May 31st. These orders were very unusual – something was brewing and our excitement, anxiety, and expectations grew. The purpose of our stop at Rota was to pick up additional personnel and provisions. The personnel included three NSA civilians and three marines. All were linguists—Russian, Arab, and Egyptian. We left Rota on June 2nd and entered the Mediterranean where Soviet Navy man-of-war ships (Destroyers) began following and shadowing us—this did not look good. We seemed to be the center of attention. Dear Lord, what did we get ourselves in to? Suddenly our causal cruise was getting very serious. Without a Destroyer escort, we would be sitting ducks because we could not defend ourselves. Remember the cold war era and the never ending military games with the Soviets were constant. Nevertheless, we sailed into the Mediterranean as fast as our WWII ship could manage.

Our orders located us at an operating area off of the Sinai Peninsula, Egypt. During our journey, we became aware of the serious trouble brewing between the Arabs and Israel. As a matter of fact, we received word a war started on June 5th. Israel completely wiped out the Air Forces of Egypt, Jordan, and Syria. They also conquered Gaza and the left bank belonging to Jordan and completely occupied the Sinai Peninsula. I remember thinking this little country kicked major "butt"—thank God they are on our side. We arrived off the coast of Sinai (Port Said), the evening of June 7th. Awakening on June 8, 1967, the morning was beautiful and sunny with a light breeze.

Our skipper, Commander William McGonagle, was concerned about the situation and ordered our forward .50 caliber gun mounts constantly manned. The gunners wore combat helmets and flack jackets. In addition, we observed darken ship at night which meant no light could be visible from the ship even if an outside door opened. Internal lights would automatically shut off when the door opened. The skipper sent a message to Vice Admiral Martin, Commander Sixth Fleet, requesting a Destroyer escort. We were advised, since we were flying the American ensign and sailing in international waters, no one would dare attack us especially since we were not a man-of-war. However, NSA was also concerned and told the Joint Chiefs to move the *Liberty* to at least 100 miles from shore and drafted a message to move us hopefully out of danger. This message was unbelievably misrouted and never received in time. Instead of going east, the communicators sent it west to the Philippines. The course this message took sent it around the

world and not to the *Liberty*. Murphy's Law was operating at its best—if something can go wrong, it will...and it did! I have personally confirmed within CIA communications the message was misrouted as the message is tracked continuously from one site to the next. Or maybe...this was fate?

Before I describe the attack, let me make the point the IDF attack occurred in three coordinated and planned phases—two sets of Israeli Air Force attack aircraft, three Navy torpedo boats, and Marines transported by helicopter. This effort was well planned and required detailed orders to their military personnel.

The morning of June 8th, 1967: For me, it was business as usual—electronic repair and General Quarters drills. My repair area assignment was Radio Research Room Two (RR-2) within the CT area. This room was both my repair responsibility and my General Quarters (GQ) location.

General Quarters (GQ) is an order to individuals assigning them to specific assignments and locations during an attack or catastrophic event. Therefore, when the GQ alarm sounded, you immediately went to your assigned GQ location as quickly as possible. Unless ordered by higher authority, you remained at this post.

I started my day trouble shooting a couple of units. However, during the morning, there were flights of low flying Israeli aircraft over a period of seven hours. On one occasion, I went topside to see for myself. As the plane approached at a very low altitude, a number of us waved to the Israeli

pilot who was so close we could see his face. He waved back in a friendly manner. His propeller engines were deafening as the plane raced by. Since we were close to Egypt, it was comforting to know the Israelis, our ally, were keeping an eye on us. Some of the crew were sun bathing—aggressive and war like—we were not. Picture in your mind the pilot's view of the ship with sailors scattered about the ship on beach chairs, blankets, or towels. The scene looked like something out of the pages of McHale's Navy. I returned to RR-2 and went back to work. Since my normal working area and GQ location were the same, I worked through a GQ drill following lunch.

When this drill was over, an announcement came on the public address system, the "1MC," that the Captain was very pleased with our quick response to the drill. However, in cautioning us to the seriousness of our situation and unaware of the approaching Israeli jets, he observed gun fire ashore which could be seen at a distance at El Harish. I found the Captain's words interesting so I decided to grab a smoke and a coke and go top side to see what all the fuss was about.

Shortly after 2:00 PM: I acquired a soda in the mess hall, and the 1MC enunciator indicated the mechanics were going to test the Captain's boat engine. While reaching for my coke, I heard the most dreadful noise. It sounded like something was very wrong with the engine. However, the sound I heard really came from the initial attack of three Israeli fighter jets firing rockets and their 30mm cannons. Immediately, the GQ alarm sounded and this time the

enunciator indicated "this is no drill—man your general quarters". I ran back to RR-2. It was like all hell had broken loose topside and I felt lucky to have lots of metal between me and the action before a rocket or bomb could affect my location. Nevertheless, the explosive metal to metal sounds were blood curdling. I could only imagine the carnage outside. God help the young kids manning those machine guns!

The events during the attack were chaotic and bloody. The initial jet attack killed four of the sailors manning the forward .50 caliber machine guns. The rockets blew them out of the machine gun barrier emplacements throwing body parts over the forecastle area (forward part of the ship near the bow). The subsequent jet attack mortally wounded our executive officer, Lt. Commander Phillip Armstrong and killed three additional shipmates. Other jets then arrived dropping napalm bombs port and starboard (both sides of the ship) igniting a fifty-five gallon gasoline drum. The external superstructure of this converted WWII cargo ship was engulfed in flames. Firefighters and stretcher bearers were shot at. These pilots were uncannily accurate placing rockets through the ship's port holes—one of them killing the helmsman. They were relentless in looking for targets. On one pass, Seaman Larry Weaver was spotted by an Israeli pilot trying to hide behind a stanchion (a large round metal device about two feet around used to dock the ship). Apparently, the Israeli pilot who was focused on Larry returned to take him out, shooting a rocket at him severely wounding him. The rocket opened his lower abdomen causing Larry to push his intestines back into his lower stomach and crawl into the ship for cover (Larry had thirty-four operations over the years to maintain his health).

While the attack was taking place, Radiomen and Electronic Technicians (ET) were desperately trying to establish a communications link. They were hampered by two major problems. The Israelis were jamming US Navy communications frequencies and international distress frequencies. However, alert personnel realized the jamming ceased during the jet attacks and therefore could transmit a MAYDAY during the interim. Irregardless, they could not find an operational transmit antenna. ET Petty Officer Terry Halbardier dodged machine gun and rocket fire to run a transmission line to the only antenna that was not shot off its base. Due to his heroic action, the radiomen managed to transmit our SOS to the Sixth Fleet pleading for help. It was received but unfortunately, help never arrived until the next morning. (After all these years, Terry was recently awarded a Silver Star on May 27, 2009. His citation is the only citation which names Israel as the aggressor.)

The air attack lasted twenty-five minutes. It seemed like forever. The jet attack finally ceased. The Captain looked up at the yard arm and noticed that our flag was shot down. He ordered the Signalmen to run up our holiday colors—a nine by fifteen foot American flag.

Next, the 1MC enunciator advised, "prepare for motor torpedo boat attack!" We were now being attacked by three motor torpedo boats (MTBs) flying Israeli flags. They launched four torpedoes at us one at a time; however our Captain did a masterful job avoiding them. Then the 1MC announced, "Brace for a torpedo attack, starboard side (right side)." This was it, I am going to die. I quickly sat down on

the deck and pushed myself up against equipment racks and prayed like I have never prayed before. I whispered an "Act of Contrition". The next event I will never forget as there was the loudest explosion I had ever heard. I found myself violently hurtling through the air and I then came back down like a ton of bricks. But, thank God, my tail was only bruised. The torpedo explosion came from an area just forward of us and on the other side of the ship. The ship swayed over to the left and seemed like it took forever to come back to the right and finally settled at a nine degree list to the right. Unbelievably, the ship did not sink! The lights went out throughout the ship and we had to rely on emergency lanterns scattered around the ship. Hey, we were still afloat.

The MTB torpedo opened a hole, forty by twenty-five feet, in our right side directly in the intercept and communications center killing twenty-five personnel. Attention now focused on the decks flooding below. There were almost 100 folks below in the area where the torpedo hit. Dear Lord, please help them! During the evacuation of the flooded spaces, some men were trapped under tipped equipment racks and others were wounded and unable to follow their shipmates to safety one deck above. Visibility was almost zero. A marine, Sergeant Bryce Lockwood and others distinguished themselves by acts of heroism to save as many as they could by going back down into the oil and water mixture. All the while, the water was rising and the hatch would have to be sealed. When the water reached the lip at the hatch top, they reluctantly closed it in order to maintain water tight integrity. Hold on, hold on! There was banging on the hatch. Someone was trapped!! They quickly opened it to let another sailor out.

Senior Chief Stan White then ordered us out of RR-2 as we were below the water line. If orders were given to abandon ship, we needed to be ready. Those of us in the CT intercept spaces now proceeded to a corridor on the port side on the upper level assisting the wounded as we grouped together and awaited further orders. Not knowing the extent of the torpedo damage, we thought the ship was going to sink. At the moment, we dared not go topside as the MTBs were still shooting at anything that moved.

As we gathered in the corridor near an outer door, we came upon John Spicher, our postal clerk petty officer, who was obviously wounded, a life preserver tightly wrapped around him. A medic was giving him mouth to mouth resuscitation. His chest was riddled with shrapnel. His blood was everywhere. Our medic ordered me and another CT to keep the life preserver in place and continue mouth to mouth resuscitation so he could leave to help others. Unfortunately, despite all our efforts, we could not save John and he died in my arms. My Catholic training kicked in and I baptized him whispering an "Act of Contrition" in his ear.

"Dear God, where are the Sixth fleet jets to save us!
Mother of God, please help us!"

Rounds of 40mm armor piecing shells continued along with bursts of 50 caliber machine gun fire. Suddenly, our Captain gave orders to prepare to abandon ship. Lt. Lloyd Painter opened an external hatch to see if it was safe to release the life rafts. To his chagrin, he witnessed an Israeli machine gun striking a life raft floating astern. Life rafts were now not an option as they were rendered unusable.

With steaming power intact and the fact the ship seemed to have held its own, the Captain did not give orders to abandon ship and requested engineering provide all available power. If the ship was going to sink, he wanted to be in deeper water to prevent the IDF from obtaining the *Liberty*'s secret equipment and documentation. Meanwhile, the mess hall was set up as a makeshift triage and the wounded were brought there as quickly as conditions would allow. Our ship's physician, Doctor Richard Kiepfer provided awesome medical assistance saving many lives. Some of the uninjured crew stayed to assist "Doc" following his instructions. Everyone pitched in. All the while, Doctor Kiepfer was wounded himself. He was a hell-of-a good doctor. Thank God he was there and still capable to treat our wounded.

In reflection, our wounded Captain, William McGonagle, kept us motivated with his projected confidence, professionalism, and demeanor. The crew felt with the Captain at the helm, we would survive. He was our rock. All we needed to do was obey his orders, assist the wounded and do anything and everything to keep the ship operational. We had to make it because too many of the crew were badly wounded and would never survive time in the water for any length of time.

While awaiting further orders as we remained in the port side corridor, the 1MC warned us to prepare to "repel boarders". We could hear helicopters. I asked a Lt. Bennett if we should get weapons from the small weapons locker. He replied no; let's wait for the Captain's orders. That really made me mad. Then all of a sudden, the shooting seemed to have stopped. Some of us cautiously went outside to see what

was going on. I discovered an Israeli helicopter with troops hovering nearby. Without any fanfare, the helicopter simply departed. Fortuitously, we believe, the Israelis intercepted an invalid message indicating U.S. aircraft were on the way. Nevertheless, the Israelis terminated the attack.

Now that the attack seemed to be over, we needed to get the hell out of the area. No one seemed to be giving orders. Those of us who were not wounded either helped the wounded or took on seafaring duties. Since our radar was taken out and night coming on, I volunteered to stand a starboard flying bridge watch. I told them that I did not want to be relieved. So, with a binocular in hand, I searched the horizon. I stayed on post the rest of the evening and through the night. Dear Lord, please keep us afloat!

As morning broke, two American destroyers came out of the horizon—the USS Davies and the USS Massey. Thank God as we were still in danger of sinking. We tied up to the Davies who provided medical, engineering, and extra manpower. They also gave us sandwiches and I gladly accepted one and continued my watch as I did not know what else to do. At about 10:00 AM, I called out there was a very large ship coming out of the horizon at 3:00 o'clock relative bearing. It turned out to be the aircraft carrier USS America and as we got closer, their helicopters began shuttling some of our wounded to the aircraft carrier. It was an awesome sight as the helicopters lined up in the air awaiting their turn to hover over our bow area to lower their stretcher-like basket picking up a wounded sailor. Some were taken to the USS America and others went to the USS Little Rock (cruiser).

In retrospect, help did not arrive until **18 hours** after the attack when the *Liberty* was only **15 minutes** away from aircraft carriers USS Saratoga and USS America fighter jets. Had the light weight inner walls given way to the sea that night, the Davies and Massey would be looking for debris, bodies, and survivors.

Ironically, the first military navy ship to offer us assistance following the attack was a Soviet Destroyer who was sailing nearby and saw the blackened and listing *Liberty* and radioed their willingness to help. Because of the cold war, we had to turn them down.

In order to completely understand that the Israeli attack was deliberate, we have obtained the following evidence. We have learned that an US Air Force security Group intercept aircraft was flying nearby and was **undetected** by the Israelis and the *Liberty*. The intercept aircraft had a Hebrew linguist aboard and translated in real time the conversations between the Israeli fighter jets and their ground controllers. The English translation was then transmitted to the Air Force security group network. The conversations were taped; however, NSA cannot or will not allow the tapes to be heard.

The following indicates the Israeli deceit and America's complicity. US Air Force Captain Richard Block who, as duty watch captain with the USAF 6931st Security Squadron on the Greek island of Crete, had the presence of mind to take action. Recognizing the intercepted instant translations between Israeli pilots and their controllers as important,

he took immediate action to forward the translations not only to national authorities in Washington at the highest precedence for intelligence material (CRITIC), but also to Air Force All Source Intelligence Centers around the world.

People who saw these translations were stunned by what they read, yet they were sworn to secrecy by the most stringent security restrictions and for the most part, while horrified, kept the story and their feelings to themselves for many years. Later, these people started to come forward, as recounted below.

One such analyst, Air Force Captain Stephen Forslund, was on duty as a US Air Force intelligence analyst at the 544th Air Reconnaissance Technical Wing, Offut Air Force Base, Omaha, Nebraska. Forslund eventually retired from the Air Force after twenty-six years of service, and told us the story after reading "Assault on the *Liberty*". James Ronald Gotcher, saw the same intercepts as a US Air Force Intelligence Analyst with the 6924th Security Squadron, Da Nang, Republic of Vietnam. In addition, Army Colonel Patrick Lang stated he saw the intercepted material at an advanced cryptographic logistical course at Fort Holabird, Maryland, a few months after the attack. Ambassador Dwight Porter saw a transcript of an intercepted Israeli message given to him by the Egypt CIA station chief: Israeli planes had been order by the IDF to attack the *Liberty*, but a pilot replied that it was an American ship. The order was repeated, but the pilot still insisted that he could see the American flag. He was then told harshly he had his orders: "attack it".

Chapter 3

Malta and the Navy Court of Inquiry—
The deceit begins

Following our morning rendezvous with the USS Davis, we set sail to Malta (a Mediterranean island) followed by a Navy sea going tug and, not to our surprise, a Soviet destroyer trying to obtain anything floating out of the side of our ship. I believe it took us six or seven days to reach Valetta, Malta. Living on the ship at this time was very gruesome as damage and the smell of death were everywhere. Visible blood stains were a constant reminder of our shipmates killed. The sun baked the blood into the walls and decks. We gathered every morning for muster (an attendance check and to receive orders of the day), very aware our shipmates and friends were missing and not coming back.

The *Liberty* finally went into dry dock (a facility to work on a ship below the water line). Before pumping the water out of the containment area, Navy divers slung a canvas patch around the torpedo hole to contain any bodies, body parts, and classified matter from spilling out. Eventually the Maltese ship fitters would patch every single hole including the torpedo hole, followed by paint. When finished, the *Liberty* looked on the outside as if it had never seen action.

The CTs were ordered into the classified spaces to clear bodies and classified material. A group, led by CT1 Ronald Kukal, was selected to identify the dead and place them in body bags. Another group led by Senior Chief Stan White, of which I participated, collected all classified material. For me personally, this assignment was more horrifying than the attack itself because under attack, my fear factor was high but, until now, I had not handled or observed body parts of my friends and fellow CTs "up close and personal". Remorse hit me like "a ton of bricks". I will never forget the carnage of my shipmates.

The spaces near the torpedo blast were very dangerous as everything was coated with a black oily substance since the torpedo had ruptured one of our fuel tanks. Therefore, the decks were very slippery and precarious. Holes in the floor were everywhere. Equipment racks filled with cryptographic equipment, internal walls, as well as the ship's hull, were gone. You could see daylight where the bulkhead used to be. The torpedo blast and its resulting shrapnel tore some of the bodies into small pieces, because of the black coating you became aware of the carnage only after you picked it up and handled it. As we moved from one foot to the next, we cleared all debris which may include a finger, toe, etc. I believe all of us who experienced this endeavor still have vivid memories, we will never forget. We all broke down at one time or another.

Finally, after all the debris was collected and bagged, most CTs were transferred to Norfolk, Virginia at which time we were given our new future assignments. A small

contingent was left behind to sail the ship back to Norfolk, Virginia, after all 821 holes were patched. The ship that left Malta looked as if nothing had happened; however, it was an empty cargo ship unable to be assigned another intelligence mission ever again. In December 1970, she was sold for scrap.

The Brass Arrives

While we were in dry dock, unknown Naval Officers came aboard to conduct a Naval Court of Inquiry. For the crew, it looked very impressive. It appeared this impressive group which included an Admiral and four Naval Captains were interested in acquiring the actual facts. At this time, the crew was confident the facts were collected and the truth of the incident accurately recorded as they obtained four days of testimony. As you will see, the Naval Court of Inquiry was a **sham**.

With a Navy gag order in place to keep the crew from discussing the event with the press, friends, and family, the crew from that point on went about their lives putting the event behind them not saying a word. Military memorials that followed were in line with the White House focus which was not to indicate on any document, monument, and the like, Israel was the offending attacker.

〜

The 1967 Navy Court of Inquiry—Obstruction of Justice at the Highest Level

Shortly after the attack while we were sailing to Malta, Admiral Isaac Kidd helicoptered out to the ship to ensure the crew did not discuss the attack with waiting newsmen. He interviewed some of the crew to obtain a preliminary idea of the event. After we arrived in Malta, he chaired the Navy Court of Inquiry which included Captain Ward Boston as his legal counsel. Selected crew members were asked to give testimony under oath. Some discovered later that their testimony of the IDF machine gunning stretcher bearers and life rafts were absent from the finished product. It became obvious the inquiry was to be completed as quickly as possible. We later learned the testimonies of the wounded on the USS America and USS Little Rock (a cruiser and Sixth Fleet Flag Ship) were considered important by the court but were over-ruled by Admiral McCain in London. They also wanted to interview Israelis however; McCain insisted the court conclude their staged and bogus court as soon as possible. We later learned that critical testimony given was removed from the final report. Members of the crew who gave testimony obtained a copy of this report and they indicated that their testimony was left out if it indicated Israeli brutality.

On June 18th, the report went to London for review and signature of Commander U.S. Naval Forces, Europe, Admiral John McCain, Jr. The process would normally include official approval of his legal counsel, Captain Merlin Staring. As Capt. Staring completed this review, he found the

"Finding of Fact" was not supported by evidence in the record. On the day he received the report, Staring worked late into the night going home only to shower, clean up, and return to his office to continue the review. Captain Boston visited Staring the next mid-morning to determine the status. Staring indicated he was not finished and he found the report hasty, superficial, incomplete, and a totally inadequate inquiry. In other words, the cited facts did not support the report's conclusion. Admirals McCain and Kidd quickly had the report taken from him denying Capt. Staring of his approving signature. Obviously, Admiral McCain, Jr. approved it as it was forwarded to Washington. Admiral McCain's action is significant, suspicious, unusual, and interesting since his legal council had reason to object and take issue with this very important document as thirty-four Americans were killed, 174 wounded, and an intelligence ship taken out of service.

Not surprising, the outcome of the report sided with an internal Israeli investigation that the attack was a terrible **accident**—a mistake that sometimes happens during the fog of war. From the very beginning the crew began to be suspicious because the actual facts the crew experienced did not make sense with statements coming out of the Johnson administration. For instance, with twelve over-flights, how could the Israelis not know who we were? Unaware of the specific details acquired by the Naval Inquiry, most of the crew were puzzled but had faith in our Navy superiors. I trusted our government would do the right thing. Could you imagine if you had a loved one on board and found the incident was now being swept under the rug?

Years latter when the crew could obtain a copy of the Inquiry report, it was discovered the Inquiry report did not make any sense to us. The Inquiry report was **deliberately falsified** to compliment the Israeli story, as stated by the Navy Court of Inquiry legal counsel, now deceased, Captain Ward Boston, Ret., in a sworn affidavit stated details acquired, were either changed or erased, so that the Israeli version indicated the attack was a tragic mistake. According to Capt. Boston, the orders to falsify came from the White House. After a couple of weeks went by following the attack, Rear Admiral Kidd told Boston, *"Ward, they aren't interested in the facts. It's a political issue and we have to put a lid on it. We've been ordered to shut up."*

⤸

Declaration of the late Ward Boston, Jr., Captain, JAGC, USN (Ret.):

"I, Ward Boston, Jr., do declare that the following statement is true and complete:

1. *For more than 30 years, I have remained silent on the topic of USS Liberty. I am a military man and when orders come in from the Secretary of Defense of the United States, I follow them.*

2. *However, recent attempts to rewrite history compel me to share the truth.*

3. *In June of 1967, while serving as a Captain in the*

Judge Advocate General Corps, Department of the Navy. I was assigned as senior legal counsel for the Navy Court of Inquiry into the brutal attack on USS Liberty, which had occurred on June 8th.

4. *The late Admiral Isaac C. Kidd, President of the Court, and I were given only one week to gather evidence for the Navy's Official investigation into the attack. Despite the fact that we both estimated that a proper Court of Inquiry into an attack of this magnitude would take at least six months to conduct.*

5. *Admiral John S. McCain, Jr., then Commander-in-Chief, Naval Forces Europe, at his headquarters in London, had charged Admiral Kidd (in a letter dated June 10, 1967) to "Inquire into all pertinent facts and circumstances leading to and connected with the armed attack; damage resulting therefore from; and deaths and injuries to naval personnel."*

6. *Despite the short amount of time we were given, we gathered a vast amount of evidence including hours of heartbreaking testimony from the young survivors.*

7. *The evidence was clear, both Admiral Kidd and I believe with certainty that this attack, which killed 34 American sailors and injured 172 others, was a deliberate effort to sink an American ship and murder its crew. Each evening, after hearing testimony all day, we often spoke our private thoughts concerning what we had seen and heard. I recall Admiral Kidd repeatedly referring to the Israeli Forces responsible for the attack as "murderous bastards". It was our shared belief, based on the*

documentary evidence and testimony we received first hand, that the Israeli attack was planned and deliberate, and could not possibly have been an accident.

8. I am certain that the Israeli pilots that undertook the attack, as well as their superiors, who had ordered the attack, were well aware that the ship was American.

9. I saw the flag, which had visibly identified the ship as American, riddled with bullet holes, and heard testimony that made it clear that the Israelis intended there be no survivors.

10. Not only did the Israelis attack the ship with napalm, gunfire, and missiles, Israeli torpedo boats machine-gunned three lifeboats that had been launched in an attempt by the crew to save the most seriously wounded – a war crime.

11. Admiral Kidd and I both felt it necessary to travel to Israel to interview the Israelis who took port in the attack; Admiral Kidd telephoned Admiral McCain to discuss making arrangements. Admiral Kidd told me that Admiral McCain was adamant that we were not to travel or contact the Israelis concerning this matter.

12. Regrettably, we did not receive into evidence and the Court did not consider any of the more than sixty witness declarations from men who had been hospitalized and were unable to testify in person.

13. I am outraged at the efforts of the apologists for Israel in this country to claim that this attack was a case of "mistaken identify".

14. In particular, the recent publication of Jay Cristol's book, *The Liberty Incident*, twists the facts and misrepresents the views of those of us who investigated the attack.

15. It is Cristol's insidious attempt to whitewash the facts that has pushed me to speak out.

16. I know from personal conversations I had with Admiral Kidd that President Lyndon Johnson and secretary of Defense Robert McNamara ordered him to conclude that the attack was a case of "mistaken identity" despite overwhelming evidence to the contrary.

17. Admiral Kidd told me, after returning from Washington, DC, that he had been ordered to sit down with two civilians from either the White House or the Defense Department, and rewrite portions of the Court's findings.

18. Admiral Kidd also told me that he had been ordered to "put the lid" on everything having to do with the attack on USS Liberty, we were never to speak of it and we were to caution everyone else involved that they could never speak of it again.

19. I have no reason to doubt the accuracy of that statement as I know that the Court of Inquiry transcript that has been released to the public is **not** the same one that I certified and sent off to Washington.

20. I know this because it was necessary, due to the exigencies of time, to hand correct and initial a substantial number of pages. I have examined the released version of the transcript and I did not see any pages that bore my hand corrections and

initials. Also, the original did not have any deliberately blank pages, as the released version does. Finally, the testimony of Lt. Painter concerning the deliberate machine gunning of the life rafts by the Israeli torpedo boat crews, which I distinctly recall being given at the Court of Inquiry and included in the original transcript, is now missing and has been excised.

21. *Following the conclusion of the Court of Inquiry, Admiral Kidd and I remained in contact, though we never spoke of the attack in public, we did discuss it between ourselves. On occasion, every time we discussed the attack, Admiral Kidd was adamant that it was a deliberate planned attack on an American ship.*

22. *Note: Paragraphs 22 through 25 are not germane to my book.*

23. *Contrary to the misinformation presented by Cristol and others, it is important for the American people to know that it is clear that Israel is responsible for deliberately attacking an American ship and murdering American sailors, whose bereaved shipmates have lived with this egregious conclusion for many years."*

Dated: January 8, 2004 and signed Captain Ward Boston, Jr.

The Court of Navy Inquiry Report is, unbelievably, the current and official US Government public stand on the incident and they point to this document as the investigation of the incident. The White House predisposition and influence on the Navy Court of Inquiry is obstruction of justice at the

highest level. There were 291 military personnel whose rights were violated under the Uniform Code of Military Justice. If anyone of us failed to live up to the Uniform Code, we would be subject to court martial. Isn't there one Congressman who understands this injustice and will stand up for us?

In Addition

At the time of the incident, everyone involved, including anyone monitoring the Navy frequencies, were given orders never to talk about the event under penalty of fine and/or imprisonment. After talking to a number of retired Navy Radiomen on duty, either as part of the Sixth Fleet or worked at a Navy radio relay shore station, were listening and monitored the *Liberty* attack. Therefore, teams of Naval Officers were dispatched throughout the area to collect any and all copies of transmissions and have them destroyed. In addition, they instructed the Radiomen they would be in serious trouble if they ever talked about what they saw.

Events that followed began a series of governmental acts to white-wash and cover-up the Israeli attack. While the evidence the crew gave was contrary, the US supported the Israelis "accidental" claim. We all thought this was very odd and as you will see, peculiar things began to happen.

As the events are true and as accurate as I can recall, I hope you are starting to appreciate the deceit and malicious intent beginning with what the Johnson Administration perpetrated against the *Liberty* crew and the American public for pro-Israeli political purposes. And it continues today.

Chapter 4

Why Attack the Ship?

Are you still **unconvinced** the Israeli Defense Forces **deliberately** attacked a US Navy Ship?

On June 8th, 1967, six hours the morning **before** the attack, as indicated earlier, the ship was subjected to intense scrutiny by Israeli photo-reconnaissance aircraft flying as low as 200 feet. Twelve over flights were counted in our official log book. How could they mistake us for an Egyptian horse carrier? That is their stand and accepted by our government. Do you think we looked like a United States Naval vessel?

The markings on our bow and stern were typical and unique United States Navy and the Star Spangled Banner was flying from our yard arm. You would have to be either very stupid or blind to think otherwise. Furthermore, we were sailing in international waters off the Sinai coast on a clear and sunny day. We were not a man-of-war. We were lightly armed with four .50 caliber machine guns for repel boarder purposes. It would be immediately obvious to military personnel of any nation the USS *Liberty* was not a fighting ship because she lacked aggressive gun emplacements,

missile and torpedo launchers – she did have an overwhelming array of some forty antennas from stem to stern. This included a very large antenna pedestal just aft (behind) of amidships supporting a sixteen foot microwave dish pointing skyward. Another large dish antenna was located on our forecastle (the front of the ship) facing forward. The Egyptians had nothing like it so why did our Government go along with this Israeli scam?

From details I have learned over the years, I can now place some of the pieces together. As the *Liberty* made her way closer to our operating area across from the Sinai and the Gaza strip, Israeli intelligence told the American CIA Station Chief they did not want our ship around as they knew we were an intelligence ship from all of the over flights they made that morning. A message was sent to Washington telling them of the Israeli concerns. However, prior to that morning, the Pentagon had already sent a message to the *Liberty* telling us to move the ship one hundred miles away from shore. Washington thought the problem was solved. This is the message we never received as it bounced all over the world. Not knowing new orders were generated and the Sixth Fleet was in the dark about the message, the Israelis must have thought Washington was getting in their face as we continued on site, especially Moesha Dayan, the Israeli Defense Minister.

It is abundantly apparent to me they were very concerned about something we might have intercepted or what we could intercept. The IDF had a choice to make since they apparently did not want us to continue our mission.

Capturing the *Liberty* was not one of their selected choices as they possessed far greater fire power than the *Liberty*. The Israelis, without firing across our bow, without advising the USS *Liberty* to leave the area, and, without requesting our surrender, brutally attacked. The *Liberty* was a virtually unarmed vessel and not a military physical threat. Ironically, at no time did the torpedo boats request the *Liberty* surrender as did the North Koreans involving the USS Pueblo in 1968. For our close ally and friend, the IDF, this was very safe target practice. The USS *Liberty* was a wonderful chance to hone their shooting and killing skills. As indicated, the Israelis had many alternatives to choose. Because they used torpedoes, is there any doubt in your mind they wanted us to sink with all hands lost?

Without the involved governments providing us with an honest explanation, we can only come to a conclusion based on available facts. This is my observation: The 67 Arab/Israeli War began on June 5, 1967 **by Israel** as confirmed by Meir Amit, Chief of Israel's secret service, 63-68. As indicated earlier, Israel had taken out the Egyptian, Syrian, and Jordanian Air Forces and totally occupied the Sinai. Israel had complete air superiority. However, as of June 8th, Israel had not taken the Golan Heights which was included in their war plans. The ship was in the right place to intercept the fact the Israelis were moving troops from the Sinai to the Syrian boarder, leaving the west militarily vulnerable to Egypt and Jordan. If Egypt counter-attacked knowing the Israelis moved their troops to the Syrian boarder, they might be able to take the Sinai back. Secrecy was an absolute necessity for success.

No one was going to deter the Israeli war plans to include the Soviets. This included President Johnson who was pressuring them to stop their land grab and come to the peace table as the Soviets were warning him. Syria and Egypt were their client states and they were in dire straights. Both lost their Air Forces and Egypt lost the Sinai and the Gaza strip. If Israel did not comply and she continued to acquire additional Arab land, the Soviets were threatening to get into the war with paratroopers at the ready. Johnson had to get the Israelis to cease and desist; however, the Golan Heights were in her sights. The IDF had to make it very clear to both America and the Soviets; Israel was not ready for peace. The USS *Liberty* had to be silenced. Israel took the Golan Heights sending the United States a clear message for future skirmishes. We were not the close ally that we think of in today's terms – if you believe that. At the time, their use for the United States was to simply keep the Soviets at bay as stated by Meir Amit. The United States and Israel were very fortunate the Soviets did not make good on their intention with Israel invading Syria taking the Golan Heights.

Historically the press has not been our friend. However, a Chicago Tribune investigative reporter, John Crewdson decided to look into our story. To our surprise, not only did Mr. Crewdson confirm details we have known for years, but also discovered facts the crew was unaware. His article appeared on the front page of the Chicago Tribune on Oct. 2, 2007 and was carried in other papers such as the Baltimore Sun. This front page story was not carried by any other major newspaper. His conclusion was the same as ours – the attack was deliberate. His article also identified an Air

Force Security Group aircraft flying nearby and recorded the Israeli fighter pilots conversations as identified earlier.

According to James Bamford in his book "Body of Secrets, chapter 13, Blood," the Israeli troops in the Sinai were also committing genocide by massacring 1,000 Egyptian prisoners of war near our location.

With the above in mind, unless the Israeli and/or our government tells us the truth, we will never know "why" Israel deliberately attacked the *Liberty*. As eye witnesses, we know the details of the attack and logical deduction can lead us to a conclusion. With that said, I am certain the *Liberty* was an impediment to their war plans as confirmed by White House Historian Doctor Tony Wells. His secrecy oath prevents him from giving us further details and I respect his "secrecy oath". See chapter nine.

For years the *Liberty* crew thought Israel tried to sink the *Liberty* with all hands lost to blame the attack on Egypt. If the ship did sink that would be a secondary benefit to the real reason. I can say for certain that concept cannot be completely true because on June 8th, 1967, Egypt did not have an air force let alone motor torpedo boats or any other vessels to launch torpedoes especially at our location. Israel had taken the Sinai and therefore our location was miles from any Egyptian controlled land. I only mention this because I have seen this idea cited in the media including the BBC movie, "Dead in the Water". At the time the movie was made, we did not have all the details we possess today. The point is I do not believe the Johnson Administration

conspired with Israel to attack the *Liberty* and blame it on Egypt. On the other hand, Israel would have benefited had Johnson thought the attackers were the Egyptians. And Johnson may have conspired with Israel to sink the *Liberty* for other reasons that someday will be known. The only problem is the Soviets were monitoring the attack and very aware of the violence and the specific details.

Chapter 5

Events that have occurred over the Years

"There is something rotten in the state of Denmark"— Shakespeare

Is it possible the following could take place in the United States of America in this day and age? Are we a nation of laws? I have not embellished what you are about to read.

Ironically, the *Liberty* crew did not know anything was amiss until 1987. Up until then, I personally thought the attack was accidental because Washington's position was based on the Navy Court of Inquiry. I trusted the White House and the Navy. Had I known of the treacherous particulars of our 1967 government; I would not have continued my intelligence career. However, I am pleased I experienced the Central Intelligence Agency as my career which taught me there are American patriots then and now deployed throughout government working hard and striving to do the right thing while protecting American lives.

The crew also discovered many senior Washington officials at that time knew the attack was deliberate and were very angry nothing was done. While the situation was bad,

it was made worse because Congress, as required by our Constitution, refuses to investigate the attack. Thus, regarding our Middle East policies, our tripartite form of government of checks and balances stopped working with the Johnson Administration. Current reality indicates honest debate will not take place if there is any chance it will result in negativity toward Israel.

As stated, Congress never conducted its own investigation of the incident. The House has a constitutional mandate to "define and punish Piracies and Felonies committed on the high seas and offenses against the Law of Nations (Article 1, section 8). To make my point, Congress investigated the attacks on the USS Stark and the USS Cole. Had they investigated the *Liberty* incident, they would have realized the *Liberty's* cover story was blown (to hide its real spy mission to the public and the world) and other Navy unarmed intelligence ships were now vulnerable to any hostile government. This point was very evident to the *Liberty* crew as we discussed it in Malta amongst ourselves. It did not take rocket science to come to this conclusion from what we just experienced. It is my conjecture if Congress investigated our attack, the USS Pueblo incident may not have occurred in January 1968 (The North Koreans killed a sailor, captured the Pueblo, and incarcerated the crew for one year and have never returned the Pueblo to us). As a matter of fact, the Pueblo skipper told us the Navy lied to him about the USS *Liberty* events. Had he known about the details, he would have refused to sail without a Destroyer escort.

Not to our surprise, our contact with Congressmen for

the most part over the years has been very disappointing—never producing any help to open an investigation. While they were cordial, few have come to our assistance. In some cases, they tried to tell us a number of congressional investigations took place. That statement is nothing but smoke and can be easily disproved at the Congressional Archives. Most importantly, no government official has ever questioned the crew under oath other than the fraudulent Naval Court of Inquiry.

In addition, our distracters claim that 11 congressional investigations have taken place. If you check the Congressional Information Service, Indexes to Congressional Hearings (both published and unpublished), and the Public Documents Master file, you will not find any evidence Congress ever launched an investigation. We have been informed one Congressional committee whose conference was classified, discussed the attack and remains classified. Please remember that whatever was discussed did not involve the crew and was a mere discussion. How can you have an investigation without the testimony under oath from the eye witnesses – the *Liberty* crew? I find this very interesting since our government agrees with Israel the attack was an accident. So what would be the harm?

Some of the crew took it upon themselves to acquire as much information as possible to learn exactly what happened. That is, they requested information through the "Freedom of Information Act' and received documents so redacted (blacked out) they lacked any intelligent information. It was obvious the events of that day were going to

be very controlled. The crew began to wonder, if the attack was an accident, why classify and keep so many documents from the crew and the public?

In 1995, as a Central Intelligence Agency Staff Officer, I sent a Freedom of Information request and received about eight inches of documents most of which were redacted. With my extensive classified clearances, Top Secret/SI Crypto, I was surprised how much was unreadable, however, as with any good intelligence organization; my security mangers decided "I did not have a need to know". However, they did provide me with a copy of the '67 Navy Court of Inquiry. To my surprise, Lt. Lloyd Painter's testimony regarding the machine gunning of our life rafts was not there. In addition, the White House lawyers removed a detailed written statement provided to the Court by the Officer of the Deck of the Morning Watch. The White House lawyers also removed written testimony provided to the Court by sixty-five *Liberty* crewmen.

The circumstances presented the Navy with a dilemma. As an example, the USS Liberty skipper, Captain William McGonagle was awarded the Medal of Honor. His award was given to him not by President Johnson at the White House which was the custom – very odd. The Captain's medal was presented to him by the Secretary of the Navy at a low level Washington Navy Yard ceremony and his citation lacked any mention of an Israeli attack. Obviously the press was not invited. In addition, Headstones at Arlington cemetery and other government official documents gave tribute to the souls at rest but did not indicate the campaign that killed them.

James Ennes – "Assault on the *Liberty*"

In 1979, survivor James Ennes, a Lieutenant at the time of the attack, wrote and published a book entitled "Assault on the *Liberty*" based on his research and investigation. The information he learned further convinced the *Liberty* crew an Israeli cover-up was taking place. With the book in hand, the USS *Liberty* Veterans Association (LVA) came together and the crew then began to compare notes and experiences. Jim became the father of the LVA. The crew now realized with the publishing of Jim Ennes' book, the dire warnings of "fine and imprisonment" had been dropped. It was now possible to talk about the attack. While remaining law abiding, the crew was agitated and determined to see the truth be told at all costs within the limits of the law. That became our mission statement – to see the truth told about the attack to the American public.

The Twentieth Reunion

A bomb shell came to light during the 20th reunion from Commander Dave Lewis, our security group senior officer. Sometime after June 9th, 1967, Mr. Lewis, who was wounded and convalescing on the USS America, was visited by Rear Admiral Raymond Geis, Sixth Fleet Carrier Division Commander. Because he knew there would be a cover-up, Admiral Geis requested Mr. Lewis never disclose the following facts until after his death and Mr. Lewis kept his promise.

That is, Admiral Geis told Mr. Lewis he responded to our MAYDAY and launched planes from the USS America

and the USS Saratoga to come to our aid and then advised the White House. Please keep in mind, the Sixth Fleet did not know who our attackers were. During the fighter attack, we could not tell them because we did not know.

The morning before the attack, the Israelis contacted our Tel Aviv embassy and indicated to have the ship move away from the area. The embassy then sent a "Criticom" message to the President. Keep in mind the Pentagon and NSA sent a message to the *Liberty* to move 100 miles from shore which was never received and they did not know that. In addition, the Air Force Security Group aircraft flying nearby also sent a Criticom message indicating the Israeli fighter jets were about to attack the *Liberty*. Secretary of Defense, Robert McNamara, recalled the aircraft and did not indicate "why" and Admiral Geis complied. The Sixth Fleet was astonished as they were unaware the attackers were Israeli. An American Navy vessel is under attack by unknown forces and they were told to stand down?

After listening to our continuing plea for help, Admiral Geis challenged the order to recall all fighter aircraft (as was his right and responsibility in this situation). He stated he ordered a second set of fighter aircraft to be launched and again informed the White House. He emphatically told them the planes were now conventionally configured just in case they thought that might be an issue. After all, the attackers could be Soviets. This time President Johnson recalled the aircraft and said, "I don't care if the ship sinks; I will not have my ally embarrassed". This comment was confirmed by Chief Petty Officer J.Q. Tony Hart stationed at the Navy's

relay station in Morocco who over-heard the conversation. It is my deduction the Criticom message from both the embassy and the Air Force aircraft told the White House the Israelis were more than just concerned and therefore Johnson and McNamara knew the attackers were Israeli and did not tell the Sixth Fleet.

Based on the fact we know Johnson and McNamara knew the attackers were Israeli, I leave it up to you to draw your own conclusion of what motive was operating as they prevented Sixth Fleet Aircraft from coming to our assistance. We were still in danger of sinking and the planes could have played a life saver role just in case the bulkheads (internal walls) gave way and the ship flooded and sank. Please remember, we did not meet up with another American Navy ship until 5:00 AM the next day. We were left on our own for eighteen hours when the Sixth Fleet jet aircrafts were just fifteen minutes away. President Johnson abandoned the USS *Liberty* under fire. We will never completely know who, what, when, and where unless an honest and objective investigation is done and a time line examined. Ironically, as stated earlier, the first military ship to ask us if they could render assistance was Soviet.

As we gathered at our reunions, we became aware we were not alone in our belief the attack was no accident. Over thirty prominent government officials agree. Included in this list is Admiral Thomas Moorer, USN, Ret., former Chairman of the Joint Chiefs. He became my friend and my inspiration—never give up this fight for the truth.

He was extremely vocal and stead-fast in his support for us right up to his last breath. He actually mentioned his support for the *Liberty* crew to his close friend Rear Admiral Mark Hill (USN, Ret.) on his death-bed.

Department of State

Many attempts to spin the attack have occurred over the years. On one such event, the Department of State convened a discussion panel in January, 2004, in order to dispel any misconceptions about the US involvement during the 1967 Arab/Israeli Six Day War.

The host was Marc Susser, State Historian. Initially, speakers explained Americas' involvement in the war to include Ambassador David Satterfield (Department Assistant Secretary of State for Near East Affairs), Harriet Schwar (Office of State Department, Historian Editor), and David Robarge (CIA Historian). Then the discussion switched to the attack on the *Liberty*. The presenters were David Hatch (Center for Cryptologic History Technical Director, NSA), Judge Jay Crystal (author), James Bamford (author), Michael Oren (Israeli author), and one other Israeli author.

Judge Jay Crystal's presentation was interesting as he must have known he was going to take criticism for his pro Israeli book, "The Liberty Incident: The 1967 Attack on the U.S. Navy Spy Ship" from Mr. Bamford as he had in his possession Captain Ward Boston's sworn affidavit. He tried to smear Captain Boston which in my opinion did not work. James Bamford gave a very compelling speech in support of

the *Liberty* crew and reminded the participants no one from the crew was invited to speak however two Israeli authors were. He also made a very important fact that the *Liberty* incident was not adequately or properly investigated by our government. He added by accepting Israel's investigation of the attack, is like asking Enron to provide details of their failure. To the shock of the State organizer, he then read the aforementioned Captain Ward Boston's sworn affidavit. Nevertheless, Hatch, Crystal, and the two Israeli authors all provided details indicating the attack were accidental.

Some of the USS *Liberty* crewmen were in the audience and upon completion of the discussion; one of the crewmen, Phil Tourney, was given a microphone and allowed to speak. Once the State Department officials realized the crewman was a *Liberty* survivor and elaborating facts which were germane to the event and not in accordance to their subversive aim, turned Phil's microphone off and quickly terminated the meeting. The common denominator: Keep the crew from participating and identifying the *Liberty* attack to this esteemed audience. Why? What were they worried about?

Rear Admiral Merlin Staring

At another event, Rear Admiral Merlin Staring (USN, Deceased.) formally requested the current Navy Judge Advocate General review the USS *Liberty* incident, Staring's document methodically listed blatant legal errors in the 67 Navy Court of Inquiry as it was rushed to be completed by the White House. Remember he was Admiral McCain's

legal counsel in London in June 1967. His focus was not that the document became falsified at a later date, but on legal JAG regulations which covers these important matters especially since thirty-four Americans had been killed and the destruction of a ship of the line. The 67 Navy Court of Inquiry lacked the thoroughness it deserved. It currently is a blight on the JAG historical record. His formal efforts fell on deaf ears as they indicated a new court of inquiry would be considered "anti-Semitic."

It is hard for me to believe the Navy JAG service's code of ethics has become so diminished. Or, possibly they do not have any choice to correct this miscarriage of justice because they are being directed by the White House. (I hope you can see political correctness is operating at its best. Is this the Soviet Navy?)

The Pentagon

The naming of a Navy ship—USS *Liberty*—is a reason for concern. That is, the Navy is building new littoral Destroyers identified as Littoral Combat Ships (LCS's). The Navy Times indicated LCS-2 was to be named the "USS *Liberty*". It did not take long for senior Navy officials to withdraw the *Liberty* title because of political concerns. LCS-1 and LCS-2 were named Freedom and Independence, respectively. Apparently, the word "*Liberty*" causes senior Pentagon officials political concern, uneasiness, apprehension, and grief rather than pride and patriotism. The Pentagon abandoned their original idea of assigning LCS's patriotic names. Why? More political correctness? This brings to mind, "a rose by

any other name is still a rose".

Doesn't the Navy know that the USS *Liberty*, AGTR-5, is the most decorated ship for a single engagement? What the hell did the crew of the USS *Liberty* do to be treated this way? We are damn proud we saved our wounded from dire consequences and the ship. Why shouldn't we be treated as the "bench mark" for determination and tenacity instead of trouble makers? If they will not name a ship "USS *Liberty*," why not name a ship "Captain William McGongale," a Medal of Honor recipient? In any case, the Pentagon is making a tragic mistake for keeping the *Liberty* at arms length. The *Liberty* crew "gets it".

News Media

The news media also distanced themselves from our attempts. Over the years, the crew began experiencing incidents which indicated the news media either only wanted to side with Israel or curtail any evidence negatively damning Israel. Their political correctness has been deafening. For example, it happened to me and a Washington, DC, news anchor, Gordon Peterson, a former marine. Gordon met with me and three other *Liberty* survivors. He wanted the true story to be told to include a special half hour show. Gordon was very taken by our story. However, after his station management reviewed his idea and saw the film, he was only allowed to mention it during the evening news and his footage was cut to a couple of actual air time minutes. It has been very obvious the door was firmly closed to assist us to obtain public support.

In addition, there have been news media covering our reunions. One such occasion, reporters and film crew from "Night Line" interviewed the crew and our memorial service. We could tell our reunion emotionally affected them. In addition, their effort must have cost Night Line a few thousand dollars to fund a film crew as there were air fare, hotel rooms, extra air baggage costs and meals. And there have been others—which all found themselves on the editors cutting block. Needless to say, the Night Line USS *Liberty* segment was never televised.

Senate Arms Services Committee

On October 4, 2006, a group of USS *Liberty* supporters were invited to meet with the legal councils for the Senate Arms Services Committee (Senior Council: Scott Able, Senator Warner Council: Dick Walsh, and Senator Carl Levin: Peter Levine). Our group included Rear Admirals Mark Hill and Merlin Staring, USN, Ret., Colonel Barrett Taylor, USAF, Ret., Ms. Pat Roushaks (widow of NSA civilian Allen Blue), and me. Our testimonies were not taken under oath. Senator Warner, who was a friend to both Admiral Staring and Colonel Taylor, was not in attendance. We were instructed that the Senate councils wanted us to provide them with evidence lacking in the 67 Court of Inquiry. They were looking for proof the Israeli attack was deliberate. Each of us provided testimony from different slants. Senator Warner's council, Dick Walsh told us after the meeting, we provided a wealth of good information. It appears Senator Warner did not want to be bothered after all. When Senator Warner was briefed by them, he stated he was just one Congressman

among many but more importantly he stated friends of his were in place when the *Liberty* was attacked and if he did anything, he felt they would feel like he was stabbing them in the back.

New York & Connecticut Speaking Engagements

In September 2008, my shipmate, Richard (Rocky) Sturman (a Radioman) and I went on a speaking engagement in New York and Connecticut. I believe there were five different locations. USS *Liberty* supporters planned the events and made the appropriate reservations in the halls and churches for our speeches. Our presence, for the most part, was well received except for Suffern, New York.

The event in Suffern was held in a large room within a library building. The populace of Suffern is primarily Jewish. I remember driving past many stores and businesses with advertisement in Yiddish – I can tell you that put lots of butterflies in my stomach. Our room was filled to capacity. As I started my presentation, I noticed about twenty veterans dressed in leather jackets embellished with campaign and service related patches. I indicated to my audience how pleased I was fellow veterans were present. Little did I know they would be a source of trouble as they were Jewish American War Veterans bent on disrupting our presentation.

In addition, while we gave our presentation, we had pictures of the wounded and gruesome damage to the *Liberty* projected behind us. As Rocky and I spoke, anything we

said that was in the least bit critical of Israel, someone would
challenge us or make a derogatory comment. For example,
I indicated Israel fired the first shot which started the war
on June 5th by attacking Egypt, Jordan, and Syria Air Forces.
They yelled "untrue"! They said President Nasser started the
war by closing the Straights of Hormuz. Nevertheless, Israel
fired the first shot "period". Obviously, Israel could not be
portrayed as the "bad guys" to these people.

I told them that Israel dropped five torpedoes in the
water and the ship was struck with one thereby they were
attempting to murder 294 Americans. This could not be! A
Jewish lady immediately replied that Israel was **not** trying
to sink the ship because if they wanted the ship to sink they
would have used a larger torpedo.

As our program continued the War Veterans were
becoming more and more belligerent and vocal. A shouting
match ensued between folks wanting to hear our presentation and them. We could not continue. The event manager
then warned the War Veterans. He anticipated trouble and
six local police officers were in the building at his request.
He asked the War veterans to leave or he would summon the
officers. The War Veterans got up and left in mass. As they
were going out the door, the last War Veteran, an elderly
former marine who, small in stature (I estimate that he was
in has late eighties), turned to Rocky and I and gave us "the
finger" as he went through the doorway. I could not believe
what I just witnessed – a former marine would be so crude
to a fellow American veteran respectfully telling the truth
and detailing the attack. Rocky and I never mentioned

anything derogatory about Jews or present day Israel and this is the way they treated us? This event was captured by the local Jewish press and Rocky and I are now in the Anti-Defamation League web site as anti-Semite and conspiracy theorists. We also made the local Jewish press. The articles identified us and our presentation as "inflammatory". We had to be trouble makers.

Presently I am not surprised that these Jews were so protective of Israel. In addition to our biased news media, I have learned from other Jewish friends that at the time of the attack, Rabbis were telling their parishioners Israel could not have possibly **deliberately** attacked an American ship. They would not dare attack their good friend's ship. I guess they want everyone to believe Israel is doing God's work. They have been duped also.

Another comment made citing the USS *Liberty* was a "spy ship". We were wrong spying on Israel and we deserved what we got. I would remind this mind set the *Liberty* never received the message to move 100 miles off shore and we thought our location was where the Pentagon needed us. Johnson was prepared to warn Israel should we discover Soviets flying their enemy's planes or any other hostile acts against Israel if the *Liberty* discovered them. Unfortunately, we did not.

Chance Meeting

On June 8th, 2009 at Arlington Cemetery an event occurred that caused my wife Patricia and I pause and

concern. We parked our car in section thirty-four and started to walk to the ceremonial headstone where six of my shipmates are buried – that is, parts of their bodies that could be collected. We approached a very soiled and very used automobile with an elderly gentlemen sitting inside and not making any attempt to accompany the group gathering at the tombstone. I went over to him and asked if I could help. Would he like to join us? He declined indicating he had problems with his legs as there was a sharp incline which would not allow him to overcome the rise. We introduced ourselves in a friendly manner and exchanged business cards. He told me he was very proud of the USS *Liberty* crew and he came to pay his respect from his car. He said he was very upset the Israelis got away with murder. I thanked him for his service to America as he was a WWII veteran who also saw action. As the memorial service continued, I glanced at the gentlemen to see if he remained and to see if he was okay. When the service concluded, the WWII veteran drove off.

On June 11th, the media reported an "elderly gentlemen" had shot his way into the Washington, DC Holocaust Museum killing a security guard. I could not believe my eyes as the "elderly gentlemen" was James Wenneker von Brunn, the same man Patricia and I met at the cemetery. One has to wonder about a man who would act on his anger and kill someone — we were inches from one another. What if he was a fanatical Israeli supporter bent on taking out the USS *Liberty* crew and their families? Doesn't our government realize by lying about the attack, it makes the USS *Liberty* crew controversial to some people and our yearly

memorial service at Arlington Cemetery a target for these same crazies? Mr. von Brunn died on January 6, 2010 awaiting trial. May God have mercy on his soul.

Christians Supporting Israel

While I cannot remember specifically the date the following occurred, nevertheless, it is worth telling.

At one of our USS *Liberty* reunions in Washington, DC, I was asked to come to a well established Protestant Church in Annandale, Virginia, for an interview. This church utilized a video studio transmitting religious shows on their web site. The pastor wanted to personally interview me. However, before the taping of the interview, the pastor and I had a chance to talk in his office.

Our conversation led to current Middle East issues of the time. I stated Israel should obey UN resolutions 242 and 338 which stated they should return to their '67 borders and they should refrain from building illegal settlements in East Jerusalem. At that point, the pastor asked me if I believed in the bible and I told him yes. He then elaborated on the passage in the bible which indicates Israel must be whole again obtaining the land God gave them in order for the Second Coming of Christ (the end of the world) to occur. He asked me if I believed this would happen. I said yes, however, I told him the Second Coming of Christ included the fact Christ will judge all souls, past and present. I reminded him Christ's message of teaching our need to love God and our neighbor. Christ's definition of neighbor included loving

all gentiles unlike the Jewish religion of the time. I told the pastor I know what side I wanted to be on when Christ judges those who indiscriminately kill Palestinian women and children for the sake of Israel becoming "whole" again. He just looked at me.

Following our discussion, I was surprised the interview went well as the pastor only focused on the attack and I am very thankful for that.

Author, Ernie Gallo at Electronics "A"
School, Treasure Island, California

Capt. William McGonagole promoting
Ernie Gallo to Communications
Technician, Second Class Petty Officer

Author, Ernie Gallo entertaining
Shipmates on the USS *Liberty*

Damage to USS *Liberty* Bridge

Torpedo Hole, Starboard Side

Damage to Starboard Bridge Area

Damaged Quarter Deck with Ernie Gallo

Survivors Ernie Gallo and
Master CTM Chief, Stan White

CTM Survivors

Before Attack

USS Liberty AGTR-5

After the Israeli Attack

Chapter 6

The War Crimes Report

On June 8, 2005, with the assistance of a California lawyer and supporter, Ronald Gotcher, and Rear Admiral Merlin Staring, Ret., the USS *Liberty* Veterans Association filed a War Crimes Report with the Secretary of the Army at the Pentagon. The Department of Defense was concerned War Crimes have occurred and they failed to respond. Therefore, any war crime should follow procedures as instructed by the Department of Defense to subordinates to ensure action is taken. That is, action is then taken as published in United States War Crimes law procedures. **Breaking with their stated legal instructions,** our report was denied. We have been formally told there will not be an investigation because the matter has been thoroughly investigated in the fraudulent 1967 Navy Court of Inquiry. However, they stated no one at the Department of the Defense had any detailed knowledge of the '67 Navy Court of Inquiry.

The following is our War Crime Report:

This report of war crimes committed against U.S. military personnel is submitted to the Honorable Secretary of the Army in his capacity as Executive Agent for the Secretary of Defense, pursuant to Department of Defense Directive Number 5810.01B (29 March 2004).

This Report is filed by the USS *Liberty* Veterans Association, Inc. a California non-profit corporation, recognized by the Internal Revenue Service as a Section 501(c)(3) tax exempt veterans organization, acting on behalf of the surviving crewmembers of USS *Liberty*.

BACKGROUND

On June 8, 1967 while patrolling in international waters in the Eastern Mediterranean Sea, USS *Liberty* (AGTR-5) was savagely attacked without warning or justification by air and naval forces of the state of Israel. Of a crew of 294 officers and men (including three civilians), the ship suffered thirty four (34) killed in action and one hundred seventy three (173) wounded in action. The ship itself, a forty million ($40,000,000) dollar state of the art signals intelligence (SIGINT) platform, was so badly damaged that it never sailed on an operational mission again and was sold in 1970 for $101,666.66 as scrap. Israel acknowledged the following facts without qualification:

a. *USS Liberty was an American ship, hence a neutral vis-à-vis the June 1967 war between Israel and its Arab neighbors.*

b. *USS Liberty remained in international waters at all times on June 8, 1967.*

c. *The attacking Israeli forces never made a positive identification of the nationality of USS Liberty before unleashing deadly force in their attack on the ship.*

At approximately 0600 hours (all times local) on the morning of June 8, 1967 an Israeli maritime reconnaissance aircraft observer reported seeing "a US Navy cargo type ship," just outside the coverage of the Israeli coastal radar defense net, bearing the hull markings "GTR-5." This report, made to Israeli naval HQ, was also forwarded immediately to the Israeli navy intelligence directorate.

Throughout the remainder of the day prior to the attack, Israeli reconnaissance aircraft regularly flew out to USS *Liberty's* position and orbited the ship before returning to their bases in Israel. A total of no fewer than eight (8) such flights were made. At approximately 1050 hours, the naval observer from the early morning reconnaissance flight arrived at Israeli air force HQ and sat down with the air-naval liaison officer there. The two officers consulted *Janes' Fighting Ships* and learned that the ship reported earlier in the day was USS *Liberty*, a United States Navy technical research ship. From 0900 hours on June 8, 1967, until the time of the attack five hours later, USS *Liberty* maintained a speed of approximately five knots and a generally westerly northwesterly course.

At 1400 hours, while approximately 17 miles off the Gaza coast, USS *Liberty's* crew observed three surface radar contacts closing with their position at high speed. A few moments later, the bridge radar crew observed high speed aircraft passing over the surface returns on the same heading. Within a few short moments, and without any warning, Israeli fighter aircraft launched a rocket attack on USS *Liberty*. The aircraft made repeated firing passes, attacking

USS *Liberty* with rockets and their internal cannons. After the first flight of fighter aircraft had exhausted their ordinance, subsequent flights of Israeli fighter aircraft continued to prosecute the attack with rockets, cannon fire, and napalm. During the air attack, USS *Liberty's* crew had difficulty contacting Sixth Fleet to request assistance due to intense communications jamming. The initial targets on the ship were the command bridge, communications antennas, and the four .50 caliber machine guns, placed on the ship to repel boarders. After the Israeli fighter aircraft completed their attacks, three Israeli torpedo boats arrived and began a surface attack about 35 minutes after the start of the air attack.

The torpedo boats launched a total of five torpedoes, one of which struck the side of USS *Liberty*, opposite the ship's research spaces. Twenty-six Americans, in addition to the eight who had been killed in the earlier air attacks, were killed as a result of this explosion. Following their torpedo attack, the torpedo boats moved up and down the length of the ship (both the port and starboard sides), continuing their attack, raking the ship with cannon and machine gun fire. In Malta, crewmen were later assigned the task of counting all of the holes in the ship that were the size of a man's hand or larger. They found a total of 861 such holes, in addition to "thousands" of .50 caliber machine gun holes. Survivors report that the torpedo boat crews swept the decks of USS *Liberty* with continuous machine gun fire, targeting communications equipment and any crewmembers who ventured above decks. Damage control firefighters, who had already risked their lives merely by appearing on

deck, had to abandon their efforts because their fire hoses had been shredded by machine gun fire. Survivors also report that the torpedo boat crews fired on the inflated life boats launched by the crew after the captain gave the order "prepare to abandon ship." This order had to be rescinded because the crew was unable to stand on the main deck without being fired upon and the life rafts were destroyed as they were launched.

The defenseless crew, initially unable to report their plight or summon assistance and with only themselves to rely upon, fought heroically to save themselves and their ship. In recognition of their effort in this single action, they were ultimately awarded, collectively, one Medal of Honor, two Navy Crosses, eleven Silver Stars, twenty Bronze Stars (with "V" device), nine Navy Commendation Medals, and two hundred and four Purple Hearts. In addition, the ship was awarded the Presidential Unit Citation.

By patching together different systems, the ship's radio operators had ultimately been able to send a brief distress message that was received and acknowledged by United States Sixth Fleet forces present in the Mediterranean. Upon receipt of that message the aircraft carriers USS *Saratoga* and USS *America* each launched aircraft to come to the aid of USS *Liberty*. The reported attacking aircraft were declared hostile and the rescue aircraft were authorized to destroy them upon arrival. The rules of engagement, authorizing destruction of the attackers, were transmitted to the rescue aircraft "in the clear" (i.e., they were not encrypted). Shortly after the Sixth Fleet transmission of the rules of engagement

to its dispatched rescue aircraft, the Israeli torpedo boats suddenly broke off their attack and transmitted messages asking if USS *Liberty* required assistance.

At the same time, an Israeli naval officer notified the US Naval Attaché at the American Embassy in Tel Aviv that Israeli forces had mistakenly attacked a United States Navy ship and apologized. The Naval Attaché notified the United States Sixth Fleet and the rescue aircraft were recalled before they arrived at the scene of the attack.

At about the same time as the cessation of the torpedo boat attack, Israeli attack helicopters arrived over the ship. Survivors report that the helicopters were packed with men in combat battle dress. The Captain of USS *Liberty* gave the order to "prepare to repel boarders" but the helicopters departed without attempting to land their troops. The official position of the United States of America concerning these events, as contained in a diplomatic note by Secretary of State Rusk addressed to the Israeli Ambassador is set forth, in relevant part, below:

"Washington, June 10, 1967. The Secretary of State presents his compliments to His Excellency the Ambassador of Israel and has the honor to refer to the Ambassador's Note of June 10, 1967 concerning the attack by Israeli aircraft and torpedo boats on the United States naval vessel U.S.S. *Liberty.*

In these circumstances, the later military attack by Israeli aircraft on the U.S.S. *Liberty* is quite literally incomprehensible. At a minimum, the attack must be condemned as an

act of military recklessness reflecting wanton disregard for human life. The subsequent attack by Israeli torpedo boats, substantially after the vessel was or should have been identified by Israeli military forces, manifests the same reckless disregard for human life. . . . The U.S.S. *Liberty* was peacefully engaged, posed no threat whatsoever to the torpedo boats, and obviously carried no armament affording it a combat capability. It could and should have been scrutinized visually at close range before torpedoes were fired. The Secretary of State wishes to make clear that the United States Government expects the Government of Israel also to take the disciplinary measures which international law requires in the event of wrongful conduct by the military personnel of a State."

There has been no statement in the last thirty-eight years by the United States government reversing or amending this formal position. The Israeli Defense Forces Chief Military Prosecutor, immediately following the attack, filed formal charges recommending court martial proceedings against a number of Israeli military personnel. Prior to the start of court martial proceedings, the IDF turned the matter over to an examining judge to confirm that the prosecution should go forward.

The examining judge disagreed with United States position that the attack was "an act of military recklessness reflecting wanton disregard for human life" and announced his finding that: "Yet I have not discovered any deviation from the standard of reasonable conduct which would justify the committal [sic] of anyone for trial." As a result of this

blanket absolution, no one in the Israeli government or military has received so much as a reprimand for their involvement in the attack, much less the punishment demanded by the United States ("the United States Government expects the Government of Israel also to take the disciplinary measures which international law requires in the event of wrongful conduct by the military personnel of a State").

Within 24 hours of the attack, the United States Navy convened a formal Court of Inquiry into that attack—a standard investigative procedure reserved for such serious events or circumstances. This procedure was unusual in only one respect – the President and members appointed to the Court of Inquiry by the Commander in Chief, U.S. Naval Forces, Europe (CINCUSNAVEUR), headquartered in London, were directed orally by the appointing authority to conduct and complete their investigative proceedings *within one week* — a most unusual requirement in light of the nature and magnitude of the events they were ordered to investigate. Convening initially in London, the Court proceeded immediately to the Mediterranean and conducted its inquiry both aboard USS *Liberty* as she limped under escort to Malta and in succeeding days as she lay in dry-dock there. Concluding their inquiries there, the President of the Court, with the Navy Judge Advocate General's Corps officer who had been appointed as Counsel to the Court, and with a Navy court reporter who had been assigned from the London headquarters to assist, returned to London on June 16, 1967 (eight days after the attack), with their results.

At London, the Navy court reporter supervised the final

production of a written record of the Court's proceedings and findings – a document over 600 typewritten pages in length. On the afternoon of June 17, 1967, that record of the Court's proceedings was delivered to the senior Navy Judge Advocate General's Corps officer on the CINCUS-NAVEUR staff for his review and recommendation to the appointing authority concerning his required endorsement and action upon the Court's proceedings and record. The CINCUSNAVEUR Staff Judge Advocate thus charged with that review—in full compliance and accord with standard Navy requirements and practice – turned immediately to his detailed examination and consideration of the record. He continued that process steadily into the early morning hours of June 18, 1967, then after a four-hour rest break resumed his review at 6:00 AM on June 18th. In the mid-after noon of June 18th an emissary from his Commander, the appointing authority, appeared and inquired of the Staff Judge Advocate concerning the status of his review and when it might be expected to be completed. The Staff Judge Advocate advised that he had by then read only about a third of the record—that there were many clerical and typographical flaws in the record that should be remedied before it was formally forwarded to the high governmental authorities who undoubtedly awaited it – that, more importantly, the reviewer had not yet been able to find, in the parts of the record he had so far reviewed, testimony or other evidence to support some of the Court's stated conclusions —and that he could not yet estimate when he could complete his review and recommendations but was continuing to devote himself solely to that task. The emissary from the appointing authority departed with that information, and

then returned about 20 minutes later with the message that CINCUSNAVEUR, the appointing authority, had directed him to come and get the Court's record from the Staff Judge Advocate and bring it back to the appointing authority. The Staff Judge Advocate accordingly surrendered the record to the emissary exactly as he had received it; he was neither then nor later asked for any of his work or opinions so far; and he had no further contact with the Court of Inquiry or its results at any time in his active Navy career. The records of the Navy Department reveal that the written record of proceedings of the U.S. Navy Court of Inquiry into the Israeli attack upon USS *Liberty* was formally submitted by the President of the Court of Inquiry to CINCUSNAVEUR, the appointing authority, by a written letter dated 18 June 1967, the very day that the record had been withdrawn by the appointing authority from his Staff Judge Advocate. The written record also reveals that the appointing authority, on that same day, placed upon that record of the Court's proceedings, a five-page First Endorsement, transmitting that Record to the Judge Advocate General of the Navy in Washington as required by the Navy's investigative procedures.

Mr. Secretary, it is respectfully submitted that, even based solely upon the facts and circumstances outlined above, the Navy Court of Inquiry into the Israeli attack on USS *Liberty*—the sole official investigation by the United States Government into that attack—was deficient and prejudiced, even at its outset, by the unreasonable haste imposed informally by the appointing authority. In addition, the processing of that Court's hasty result was further compromised by its peremptory withdrawal from its initial and

prescribed legal review in the field, and its hurried transmission to the seat of the U.S. Government under cover of a purported official endorsement that could not conceivably have been based upon even a cursory complete review of even the hasty work of the Navy Court of Inquiry. Inexplicably, the Court record was classified Top Secret and withheld from public scrutiny for many years.

In addition to all of that, however, the Judge Advocate General's Corps officer who was appointed to serve as Counsel to the Navy Court of Inquiry—the officer charged with certifying the authenticity of the Court's record—has examined a copy of the record of that Court of Inquiry that has since been released by the Government under the Freedom of Information Act and has pronounced it a fraud, and not the record that he had certified and submitted. Furthermore, the President of the Court of Inquiry, following his departure from London with the record on 18 June 1967, his personal delivery of the record to officials in Washington, and his return to his regular duty post in Italy, informed the officer who had served as Counsel to the Court of Inquiry that the Court's record of its proceedings had been altered, in his presence, by civilian Government attorneys following its submission. The Central Intelligence Agency issued an "interim" report on the attack, dated June 13, 1967 (five days after the attack and five days before the apparent completion of the Navy's abbreviated Court of Inquiry). The heavily redacted copy of the CIA's report that has been released to the public does not state a conclusion, but suggests that, based on the information available as of the date of the report, the Israeli forces may not have known that they were attacking an American ship.

Writing in his memoirs, Richard Helms, the Director of Central Intelligence at the time of the attack, explained that the Central Intelligence Agency undertook a "final" investigation after more evidence became available, and he offered the following information concerning the CIA's final finding: "Israeli authorities subsequently apologized for the incident, but few in Washington could believe that the ship had not been identified as an American naval vessel. Later, an interim intelligence memorandum concluded the attack was a mistake and not made in malice against the U.S. . . . .I had no role in the board of inquiry that followed, **or the board's finding that there could be no doubt that the Israelis knew exactly what they were doing in attacking the *Liberty*.** I have yet to understand why it was felt necessary to attack this ship or who ordered the attack." [Emphasis added] Director Helms was not the only administration official who remained convinced that the attack was deliberate. In 1990, in his memoirs, Secretary of State Rusk observed: "But I was never satisfied with the Israeli explanation. Their sustained attack to disable and sink *Liberty* precluded an assault by accident or some trigger-happy local commander. Through diplomatic channels we refused to accept their explanations. I didn't believe them then, and I don't believe them to this day. The attack was outrageous."

Similarly, Clark M. Clifford, Counsel to the President at the time of the attack, recalled: "I do not know to this day at what level the attack on the *Liberty* was authorized and I think it is unlikely that the full truth will ever come out. Having been for so long a staunch supporter of Israel, I was particularly troubled by this incident; I could not bring

myself to believe that such an action could have been authorized by Levi Eshkol. Yet somewhere inside the Israeli government, somewhere along the chain of command, something had gone terribly wrong—and then had been covered up. I never felt the Israelis made adequate restitution or explanation for their actions...."

The then-General Counsel for the Department of Defense, attorney Paul C. Warnke, opined: "I found it hard to believe that it was, in fact, an honest mistake on the part of the Israeli air force units. I still find it impossible to believe that it was. I suspect that in the heat of battle they figured that the presence of this American ship was inimical to their interests, and that somebody without authorization attacked it."

The Executive Branch of the United States Government undertook no further review of the attack. Similarly, the United States Congress has never investigated the attack, making it the only attack on a United States Navy ship, involving significant loss of life that has not been so investigated. Compounding the harm done to survivors was the task given to them to bring all human remains and classified materials out of the research spaces that had been destroyed by the torpedo explosion. The survivors assigned to this task were further traumatized by having to secure the remains of their shipmates, men they knew and had lived and worked with.

In the years that followed the attack, almost all of the evidence pertaining to the attack remained, inexplicably,

highly classified. Starting in the late 1970s, heavily redacted documents began to be released as a result of FOIA requests. To this day, many USS *Liberty* related documents, including the CIA report referenced by Director Helms, remain classified. A number of individuals and groups, some directly in the employ of the Israeli government, others self-appointed, have attempted to convince the public that the attack on USS *Liberty* was but an "innocent mistake." In furtherance of this goal they have fabricated and repeated demonstrably false allegations – the most notable fabrication being that there have been "thirteen official investigations (including five Congressional investigations)"—all of which concluded that the attack was a "tragic error." These allegations are wholly and demonstrably false. Worse, in some instances, deliberately falsified evidence has been proffered in support of this argument. As a result of the public relations campaign undertaken on behalf of Israel, the USS *Liberty* survivors have been vilified for their assertions that the attack was deliberate and for their ongoing quest for justice. They are characterized as "neo-Nazis," "anti-Semites," and "conspiracy theorists" for wanting nothing more than an honest, open investigation of the attack on their ship and themselves.

In 2003, an independent commission of highly regarded experts was created to look into the matter. The Commission consisted of Admiral Thomas H. Moorer, United States Navy (Ret.), Former Chairman, Joint Chiefs of Staff; General Raymond G. Davis, United States Marine Corps, (MOH), Former Assistant Commandant of The Marine Corps; Rear Admiral Merlin Staring, United States Navy (Ret.), Former

Judge Advocate General Of The Navy; and Ambassador James Akins (Ret.), Former United States Ambassador to Saudi Arabia. The *"Moorer Commission"* (Chaired by Adm. Moorer) investigated the attack and made the following findings: "We, the undersigned, having undertaken an independent investigation of Israel's attack on USS *Liberty*, including eyewitness testimony from surviving crewmembers, a review of naval and other official records, an examination of official statements by the Israeli and American governments, a study of the conclusions of all previous official inquiries, and a consideration of important new evidence and recent statements from individuals having direct knowledge of the attack or the cover up, hereby find the following:

a. That on June 8, 1967, after eight hours of aerial surveillance, Israel launched a two hour air and naval attack against USS *Liberty*, the world's most sophisticated intelligence ship, inflicting 34 dead and 173 wounded American servicemen (a casualty rate of seventy percent, in a crew of 294);

b. That the Israeli air attack lasted approximately 25 minutes, during which time unmarked Israeli aircraft dropped napalm canisters on USS Liberty's bridge, and fired 30mm cannons and rockets into our ship, causing 821 holes, more than 100 of which were rocket-size; survivors estimate 30 or more sorties were flown over the ship by a minimum of 12 attacking Israeli planes which were jamming all five American emergency radio channels;

c. That the torpedo boat attack involved not only the firing of torpedoes, but the machine-gunning of

Liberty's firefighters and stretcher-bearers as they struggled to save their ship and crew; the Israeli torpedo boats later returned to machine-gun at close range three of the *Liberty*'s life rafts that had been lowered into the water by survivors to rescue the most seriously wounded;

d. That there is compelling evidence that Israel's attack was a deliberate attempt to destroy an American ship and kill her entire crew; evidence of such intent is supported by statements from Secretary of State Dean Rusk, Undersecretary of State George Ball, former CIA director Richard Helms, former NSA directors Lieutenant General William Odom, USA (Ret.), Admiral Bobby Ray Inman, USN (Ret.), and Marshal Carter; former NSA deputy directors Oliver Kirby and Major General John Morrison, USAF (Ret.); and former Ambassador Dwight Porter, U.S. Ambassador to Lebanon in 1967;

e. That in attacking USS *Liberty*, Israel committed acts of murder against American servicemen and an act of war against the United States;

f. That fearing conflict with Israel, the White House deliberately prevented the U.S. Navy from coming to the defense of USS *Liberty* by recalling Sixth Fleet military rescue support while the ship was under attack; evidence of the recall of rescue aircraft is supported by statements of Captain Joe Tully, Commanding Officer of the aircraft carrier USS Saratoga, and Rear Admiral Lawrence Geis, the Sixth Fleet carrier division commander, at the time of the attack; never before in American naval

history has a rescue mission been cancelled when an American ship was under attack;

g. That although *Liberty* was saved from almost certain destruction through the heroic efforts of the ship's Captain, William L. McGonagle (MOH), and his brave crew, surviving crewmembers were later threatened with "court-martial, imprisonment or worse" if they exposed the truth; and were abandoned by their own government;

h. That due to the influence of Israel's powerful supporters in the United States, the White House deliberately covered up the facts of this attack from the American people;

i. That due to continuing pressure by the pro-Israel lobby in the United States, this attack remains the only serious naval incident that has never been thoroughly investigated by Congress; to this day, no surviving crewmember has been permitted to officially and publicly testify about the attack;

j. That there has been an official cover-up without precedent in American naval history; the existence of such a cover-up is now supported by statements of Rear Admiral Merlin Staring, USN (Ret.), former Judge Advocate General of the Navy; and Captain Ward Boston, USN, (Ret.), the chief counsel to the Navy's 1967 Court of Inquiry of *Liberty* attack;

k. That the truth about Israel's attack and subsequent White House cover-up continues to be officially concealed from the American people to the present day and is a national disgrace;

1. That a danger to our national security exists whenever our elected officials are willing to subordinate American interests to those of any foreign nation, and specifically are unwilling to challenge Israel's interests when they conflict with American interests; this policy, evidenced by the failure to defend USS *Liberty* and the subsequent official cover-up of the Israeli attack, endangers the safety of Americans and the security of the United States.

WHEREUPON, we, the undersigned, in order to fulfill our duty to the brave crew of USS Liberty and to all Americans who are asked to serve in our Armed Forces, hereby call upon the Department of the Navy, the Congress of the United States and the American people to immediately take the following actions:

- *FIRST: That a new Court of Inquiry be convened by the Department of the Navy, operating with Congressional oversight, to take public testimony from surviving crewmembers; and to thoroughly investigate the circumstances of the attack on the USS Liberty, with full cooperation from the National Security Agency, the Central Intelligence Agency and the military intelligence services, and to determine Israel's possible motive in launching said attack on a U.S. naval vessel;*

- *SECOND: That every appropriate committee of the Congress of the United States investigate the actions of the White House and Defense Department that prevented the rescue of the USS Liberty, thereafter threatened her surviving officers and men if they exposed the truth, and covered up the*

true circumstances of the attack from the American people; and,

- *THIRD: That the eighth day of June of every year be proclaimed to be hereafter known as USS LIBERTY REMEMBRANCE DAY, in order to commemorate USS Liberty's heroic crew; and to educate the American people of the danger to our national security inherent in any passionate attachment of our elected officials for any foreign nation.*

We, the undersigned, hereby affix our hands and seals, this 22nd day of October, 2003.

Admiral Thomas H. Moorer, USN, Ret. Former Chairman, Joint Chiefs of Staff,

General of Marines Raymond G. Davis, USMC, MOH Former Commandant of the United States Marine Corps,

Merlin Staring Rear Admiral Merlin Staring, USN, Ret., Former Judge Advocate General of the Navy,

James Akins Ambassador James Akins, Ret., Former United States Ambassador to Saudi Arabia"

The federal criminal code makes special provision for the prosecution of war crimes whether inside or outside the United States, committed against United States armed forces personnel:

"*18 United States Code, Sec. 2441. - War crimes*

(a) Offense—

Whoever, whether inside or outside the United States, commits a war crime, in any of the circumstances described in subsection (b), shall be fined under this title or imprisoned for life or any term of years, or both, and if death results to the victim, shall also be subject to the penalty of death.

(b) Circumstances—

The circumstances referred to in subsection (a) are that the person committing such war crime or the victim of such war crime is a member of the Armed Forces of the United States or a national of the United States (as defined in section 101 of the Immigration and Nationality Act).

(c) Definition—

As used in this section the term "war crime" means any conduct—

(1) defined as a grave breach in any of the international conventions signed at Geneva 12 August 1949, or any protocol to such convention to which the United States is a party;

(2) prohibited by Article 23, 25, 27, or 28 of the Annex

to the Hague Convention IV, Respecting the Laws and Customs of War on Land, signed 18 October 1907;

(3) which constitutes a violation of common Article 3 of the international conventions signed at Geneva, 12 August 1949, or any protocol to such convention to which the United States is a party and which deals with non-international armed conflict; or

(4) of a person who, in relation to an armed conflict and contrary to the provisions of the Protocol on Prohibitions or Restrictions on the Use of Mines, Booby-Traps and Other Devices as amended at Geneva on 3 May 1996 (Protocol II as amended on 3 May 1996), when the United States is a party to such Protocol, willfully kills or causes serious injury to civilians."

The Geneva Convention (1949) defines the term "grave breach" as follows: "Article 51 Grave breaches to which the preceding Article relates shall be those involving any of the following acts, if committed against persons or property protected by the Convention: willful killing, torture or inhuman treatment, including biological experiments, willfully causing great suffering or serious injury to body or health, and extensive destruction and appropriation of property, not justified by military necessity and carried out unlawfully and wantonly." Even if there were no special provision authorizing the prosecution of war crimes, the provisions of 18 U.S.C. Sec. 1114 compel the prosecution of those who kill or attempt to kill United States armed forces

personnel in the performance of their duties.

"Sec.1114. Protection of officers and employees of the United States..... Whoever kills or attempts to kill any officer or employee of the United States or of any agency in any branch of the United States Government (including any member of the uniformed services) while such officer or employee is engaged in or on account of the performance of official duties, or any person assisting such an officer or employee in the performance of such duties or on account of that assistance, shall be punished –

> (1)In the case of murder, as provided under section 1111;
>
> (2)In the case of manslaughter, as provided under section 1112; or
>
> (3) In the case of attempted murder or manslaughter, as provided in section 1113."

The prohibition against attacking neutrals on the high seas is unconditional. It does not allow for mistake. The belligerent force, when on the high seas, **must** verify that their proposed target is not a neutral and is, in fact, a co-belligerent. This provision very sensibly attempts to prevent the use of deadly force by mistake. The United States of America has long and vigorously asserted the right of its warships to transit the high seas, free from molestation by belligerents of wars to which the United States is not a party.

Of particular relevance to this matter, the *Geneva Convention (1949)* provides

"REPRESSION OF ABUSES AND INFRACTIONS

Article 51

Grave breaches to which the preceding Article relates shall be those involving any of the following acts, if committed against persons or property protected by the Convention: willful killing, torture or inhuman treatment, including biological experiments, willfully causing great suffering or serious injury to body or health, and extensive destruction and appropriation of property, not justified by military necessity and carried out unlawfully and wantonly.

Article 52

No High Contracting Party shall be allowed to absolve itself or any other High Contracting Party of any liability incurred by itself or by another High Contracting Party in respect of breaches referred to in the preceding Article."

In the instant matter, Israel freely acknowledged that USS *Liberty* was a neutral ship in international waters. Israel also admitted that the attack was deliberate and made with the intent to sink the ship and crew. Israel has thus explicitly admitted the essential elements of a violation of Article 1 of the *Hague Convention on Naval Warfare.* Israel has further admitted the essential elements required to establish a "grave

breach" as that term is defined in the *Geneva Convention (1949)*. The Nürnberg War Crimes Tribunal established certain principles that were later adopted by all members of the United Nations. Of particular relevance is Principal VI: The crimes hereinafter set out are punishable as crimes under international law:

...(b) War crimes:

Violations of the laws or customs of war which include, but are not limited to, murder, ill-treatment or deportation to slave-labor or for any other purpose of civilian population of or in occupied territory; murder or ill-treatment of prisoners of war, of persons on the Seas, killing of hostages, plunder of public or private property, wanton destruction of cities, towns, or villages, or devastation not justified by military necessity. " It is well settled that homicides resulting from the accused committing an act inherently dangerous to others and showing a wanton disregard of human life may be charged as murder: "Homicides prosecuted under Article 118(3) are those unlawful killings which result from an accuser's committing "an act inherently dangerous to others and" showing "a wanton disregard of human life." The accused must also know that death or great bodily harm was a "probable consequence" of his conduct. Not surprisingly, intentional homicides under Article 118(2) also generally involve death as a "probable consequence"; and they are most often committed by acts which are

"inherently dangerous," particularly to the deceased, and show "a wanton disregard" for the victim (*i.e.,* killing by gunfire or other dangerous weapon). We stated previously that, for unpremeditated murder under Article 118(3), Congress enacted the rule that murder by an act inherently dangerous to others requires 'a wanton disregard of human life" in general, without the actions of the accused "being aimed at anyone in particular.'"

U.S. v. Berg, *31 M.J. 38, 39, 40 (CMA, 1990).*

This is not a case of first impression. Precedent exists for the finding that this type of attack represents a grave breach of the Laws of War. Accordingly it is established, *prima facie,* that Israel was guilty of the commission of the war crime of attacking a neutral vessel in neutral waters as a consequence of its attack on USS *Liberty.* USS *Liberty* survivors, through sworn statements, have established that the Israeli torpedo boats shot at rescuers and firefighters on the deck of the ship. They have further established that the same torpedo boats shot at USS *Liberty's* life rafts, after the rafts had been put over the side of the ship into the sea for use by shipwrecked survivors. There also exists *prima facie* evidence that Israeli forces committed additional separate war crimes by firing on the wounded and their rescuers, as well as subsequently themselves of any wrongdoing, including criminal negligence, involving their attack on USS

Liberty. When provided with a copy of the Israeli report, NSA Deputy Director Louis Tordella wrote "A nice whitewash for a group of ignorant, stupid and inept [epithet redacted]" on the cover of his copy. In that Israel has abdicated its responsibility under international law to investigate and bring the wrongdoers to justice, the task falls to the government of the aggrieved parties to act on their behalf.

Conclusion

The USS *Liberty* Veteran's Association has established, *prima facie*, the commission of war crimes by the state of Israel against US military personnel and civilians. These Americans volunteered to serve their country. They followed all orders given to them. In the course of following those orders, they were suddenly and deliberately attacked by naval and air forces of the state of Israel and their country did absolutely nothing to protect them or seek justice on their behalf.

The failure of the United States government to undertake a complete investigation of the Israeli attack on USS *Liberty* has resulted in grievous harm to the surviving victims, as well as to the families of all crewmembers. Equally serious, this failure has resulted in an indelible stain upon the honor of the United States of America. It has sent a signal to America's serving men and women that their welfare is always

subordinate to the interests of a foreign state. The only conceivable reason for this failure is the political decision to put the interests of Israel ahead of those of American servicemen, employees, and veterans. Finally, the fact that the Israeli government and its surrogates in the United States have worked so long and hard to prevent an inquiry itself speaks volumes as to what such an inquiry would find. The USS *Liberty* Veterans Association, Inc. respectfully insists that the Secretary of the Army convene an investigatory body to undertake the complete investigation that should have been carried out thirty-eight years ago.

Respectfully submitted on behalf of the USS *Liberty* Veterans Association, Inc., on this, the thirty-eighth anniversary of the Israeli attack on their ship June 8, 2005

By
Gary W. Brummett, President and Member of the Board of Directors

Stan W. White...Member of the Board of Directors

Maurice Shafer...Member of the Board of Directors

Glenn Oliphant...Member of the Board of Directors

Ernest A. Gallo...Member of the Board of Directors

James R. Gotcher...General Legal Counsel

As repeated earlier for emphases, we have been formally told that there will not be an investigation because the matter has been thoroughly investigated in the fraudulent 1967 Navy Court of Inquiry. However, they have stated that no one at the Department of the Defense has any knowledge of the '67 Navy Court of Inquiry. It is more important to protect our relationship with Israel than to obey our laws supporting our citizens, our veterans, and our killed in action. If an investigation is held and these facts are determined to be honest and true, I wonder how many laws were broken by President Johnson and others. Justice must be served. America, for the sake of history and its influence on our children, this blatant non-compliance of the Defense Department, given our clear cut evidence of a War Crime, must be investigated.

Chapter 7

The Navy Leaue & the American Legion Bigotry

The Navy League of the United States vs. the Truth of the USS Liberty Attack

*N*ote: The Navy League of the United States is a great organization serving the Navy, Coast Guard, Marines, Merchant Marine, and Sea Cadets very well. At the Washington level they lobby Congress for the best equipment our nation can develop and provide for them. At the local level, the various councils do their utmost to honor exceptional service personnel and provide programs for our nation's youths (Sea Cadets). However, on occasion the proverbial "bad apple" occurs in their local leadership. Unfortunately, at the time, I also found USS *Liberty* bigotry existing at the national level otherwise the following would have never occurred. As you will come to discover, the Navy League finally came around to stop harassing Ted Turowski and I—allowing us to continue our support to our military in the Navy League.

The Story

In November 2005, I was asked to give a USS *Liberty* speech to the St. Augustine Navy League (SANL) Council and it was warmly received. The speech I gave was respectful but nevertheless controversial. However, I found mutual respect and camaraderie in the hearts of its members and I enjoyed the interaction. I liked the folks and their genuine warmth and I became an enthusiastic, productive, and loyal SANL member.

I accomplished numerous tasks during my membership. When a situation developed relating to books, I suggested and successfully initiated a program called the "Captain William McGonagle Memorial Library," named after the USS *Liberty* skipper. New and used books were gathered and distributed to SANL support components and to every ship at Mayport Naval Station, Florida. At that time, I distributed over 5,000 books. When a box of books was presented to a command, I talked openly and freely about Captain McGonagle, his Medal of Honor, and his courageous efforts to get us out of harms way. When I stated the Israeli attack was brutal and deliberate, I received some irritated comments by a few SANL members which somewhat surprised me given their original *Liberty* acceptance. None of the military commands ever complained about the USS *Liberty* story.

To my pleasant surprise, a new member joined the council. Her name was Mrs. Ginny Hoffman, the older sister of Dwayne Margraff, a shipmate killed in the attack. Dwayne and I worked together in the CT electronic repair shop

aboard the *Liberty*. His work bench was next to mine. He was more than a work mate as we spent many hours playing cards and having fun when not on duty. Ginny's husband, Bill, is a retired Communications Technician, Maintenance Divison, Navy Master Chief and Dwayne idolized him as a teenager. Dwayne joined the Navy to follow in Bill's footsteps. Ginny's SANL membership meant a lot to me as it brought reality of the Israeli attack killing American sailors such as Dwayne to the SANL membership.

From 2005, I advanced to become the military liaison to our adopted ship, USS Farragut, DDG-99. These duties included being in close contact with their skipper and Command Master Chief. As the ship identified their outstanding sailors, I would inform representatives of Senators Nelson and Martinez, and Representative Mica. They would provide statements to be inserted into their files. In addition, I would present the sailors with plaques, the city of St. Augustine gifts, and one hundred dollars from SANL.

If the skipper felt he needed help, he knew he could count on me. For example, Mayport Naval Station had a Christmas ship decoration competition. I contacted SANL members and we worked right alongside the Farragut crew hanging Christmas lights and decorations over the outside of the ship. Visiting Mayport Naval Station at Christmas is really special with all the ships brightly decorated. It is truly a sight to behold.

On another occasion, their forty-eight inch flat screen Ward Room TV came off its mounting in heavy seas. The

Farragut did not have the money to replace it and the skipper asked me if SANL could help. With the help of SANL membership, I collected the funds necessary and a replacement TV was purchased making the Farragut crew very happy. Things could not have been better as the liaison.

As a matter of fact, in December of 2009, I was presented with the SANL Presidential award and elected Vice president for Military Affairs by the membership (the number two position in the council). In addition, I **continued** to carry out my USS Farragut liaison duties and continued the Capt. William McGonagle Memorial Library project collecting used books for the military.

On January 1, 2010, a new SANL president took over, William Korach. This individual, an Israeli supporter, found my Israeli statements offensive and in February 2010 attempted to officially curtail my freedom of speech. Trouble started when I asked a question of an invited military guest who was a Middle East expert and very in tune to fanatical Islamics. Specifically, I asked, "if America stopped supporting Israel and told them to make peace with Palestine, would the fanatical Islamics continue to come after us?" Korach aggressively got up off his seat and shouted in a demeaning manner, "We will have none of that". While I did not say anything at the time, later in the meeting, Korach dressed me down in public for my anti-Israeli views and statements. In private, I demanded either he publicly apologize to me **or** I would step down from my elected position as I could not work with him under these conditions. He refused calling me anti-Semitic and eventually gave me a

choice – stop talking about the *Liberty* or be terminated. In any case, Korach did not want me as his number two man in the council and he was not about to apologize.

The following is a time line of events:

- *Prior to Mar. 4, 2010 – I met with Dave Sullivan, Northeast Florida Navy League President, at my house to discuss settling the confrontation with Mr. Korach. I pushed for this meeting as I believed if I had a chance to explain to Mr. Korach; I was not anti-Semitic and wanted to make things right between us. In doing so, I would want my positions re-instated. Mr. Sullivan indicated he would talk with Mr. Korach and pass on my ideas and the three of us should meet. However, Mr. Sullivan called me requesting that I come to a Mar. 4th board of directors meeting and the situation would be settled. I felt comfortable the problem would be resolved.*

- *Mar. 4, 2010 – Board of Directors meeting – Mr. Sullivan opened the meeting explaining the problem between Mr. Korach and me and hopefully would be settled giving me the floor. Without attacking Mr. Korach, I read a portion of an article I wrote indicating that because of the "stated accidental attack" lie; some people believe the crew to be anti-Semitic. I also stated the Eleventh Commandment, "Thou shall not criticize Israel or its supporters," again without attacking Mr. Korach. Mr. Sullivan then gave Mr. Korach the floor and he publicly called*

*me anti-Semitic and said he had found my name
on suspect web sites. I could not believe he attacked
me again. Mr. Sullivan said and did* **nothing.** *I was
furious and rather than embarrass Mr. Korach, Mr.
Sullivan, or myself, I left the meeting. I felt I had
been* **set up** *especially after the support Mr. Sullivan
had given me in the past. I expected Sullivan to do
the right thing and mediate the situation and end
the hostilities.*

Note: At no time, did I state that I resigned my positions
outright—Vice president of Military Affairs and Liaison to
the USS Farragut. My resignation was conditional which I
stated repeatedly. Wasting no time though, Korach sought
and found replacements for both positions.

- *Mar. 22, 2010 – I met with William Dudley, Navy
  League Florida President at a coffee house. We discussed all that transpired and I pleaded with him
  to talk with Mr. Korach and arrange a meeting
  between the three of us to settle this situation. FYI:
  Mr. Korach had indicated we could settle this respecting each other's position.*

- *Mar. 22, 2010 – Mr. Dudley and I exchanged emails
  regarding my understanding of the Navy League's
  mission statement.*

- *Mar. 26, 2010 – I received an email from Mr. Korach
  indicating: a willingness to meet with me; and, my
  assignment resignation was accepted at the recent
  board meeting (which I did not do).*

- *Mar. 27, 2010 – I sent an email to Mr. Korach stating that I would meet with him and either Sullivan or Dudley.*

- *Mar. 27, 2010 – I received an email from Mr. Korach indicating he would meet with me.*

- *Mar. 29, 2010 – I sent an email to Messrs. Sullivan and Dudley indicating Mr. Korach has slandered me twice and I wanted justice.*

- *April 2, 2010 – I met with Messrs, Dudley & Korach at Barnes and Noble Book Store. After a lengthy discussion, I was told that if I never spoke of the USS Liberty again and agreed to be placed on six month probation, I would be allowed to continue with SANL and keep my book project. However, my SANL leadership and Liaison position were terminated. I informed them I did nothing wrong and this arrangement was unsuitable. The meeting dissolved negatively.*

- *April 8, 2010 – received an email from Mr. Dudley indicating that in response to emails from Messrs. Sullivan & Korach, I was hereby suspended from SANL. I was also advised that by publicly indicating Israel deliberately attacked the Liberty, I was jeopardizing the Navy League's 501c(3) status because my comment was a political statement. Dudley, the all Florida president who is also the St. Johns Veterans Council Chairman, indicated if I never talk about the USS Liberty again and placed on six month probation, I could return to SANL without resuming*

to my elected position. I refused reaffirming I did nothing wrong.

- *April 12, 2010 – SANL monthly meeting – the meeting opened with Mr. Korach reading a list of charges against me and I was officially suspended. I requested a chance to defend myself, however, they said no. Mr. Ted Turowski spoke on my behalf stating I did nothing wrong and I was slandered. He also indicated he was disgusted with their attitude and the effort to terminate me.*

So, after total support since 2005, my St. Augustine membership was suddenly terminated and I was forbidden to participate in future Navy League events locally and all of Florida. Dudley, Sullivan, and Korach insured I could not speak to the SANL board of directors and the council to defend myself. In fact, while in my presence, I witnessed statements indicating I supposedly said I wanted Israel wiped off the map, I was anti-Semitic, and I was mentally sick for not supporting our ally. The SANL Chaplin told the council, as I was being drummed out at that meeting, I had PTSD and needed help.

- *April 16, 2010 – I received an email from Mr. Dudley indicating if I wanted to be reinstated I must:*

- *refrain from all political referencing to the US/Arab/ Israeli situation*

- *refrain from any extension of the USS Liberty event*

- *refrain from any political views.*

- *April 21, 2010 – received an email from Mr. Dudley indicating I had until 23 April to decide to accept the above conditions.*

- *April 23, 2010 – I sent an email to Mr. Dudley reviewing events and details. In summary, I indicated I did nothing wrong and therefore it was unnecessary for me to do anything.*

- *April 27, 2010 – I sent an email to Mr. Dudley stating I wanted justice regarding my suspension.*

In May 2010 I went to Washington, DC, for other matters and I visited Navy League Headquarters in Roslyn, VA. I requested assistance to discuss the problem at my Navy League Council. A senior Headquarters member approached me. I introduced myself and started to explain my situation. He apparently knew something about my problem because before I had a chance of addressing my problem in detail with SANL, this senior official told me I should believe the attack was accidental as they do. It appeared to me; upper level managers supported the hierarchy chain of command rather than review my past record or consider my first amendment rights. When he was finished I reminded him of the events that had taken place at SANL and as far as the *Liberty* was concerned, I was an eye witness and the attack was deliberate. It did not matter as he based his belief on a book written by a Judge Jay Crystal which indicated the attack was a case of mistaken identity which sometimes

happens in the fog of war. I told him this book was filled with lies and falsehoods and consequently he believed I was a trouble-maker. To resolve the case at hand, I was told to go back to SANL and "work it out" with the SANL board of directors. I began to wonder if the Navy League Headquarters staff all believed the *Liberty* attack was accidental. I left feeling depressed and accomplished nothing.

- *June 14, 2010 – received an email from Mr. Korach indicating my suspension was confirmed by the SANL board.*

When I sought SANL justice, I was kicked out as requested by Korach and supported by the Northeast and all Florida presidents, Messrs David Sullivan and William Dudley, respectively. Remember I was never allowed to address the board of the charges against me as stipulated by Navy League Headquarters. This suspension violated the Navy League's by-laws as this was a case of the improper use of power to circumvent a Navy Leaguer freedom of speech.

The prior SANL president and then Navy League Director, retired Chief, Ted Turowski, and another friend, Bill Sabia were viciously criticized for their support of me by Korach, Dudley, and Sullivan which resulted in Turowski's SANL council resignation. Ted Turowski was one of the most caring, active, effective, and proficient SANL members. SANL cannot dispute his documented hard work and

resourcefulness – more on him later. Their collective treatment of Ted was despicable especially since he was a Navy League Director.

While Ted Turowski and I refrained from having any association with SANL, we attended various Navy functions which were also attended by SANL members. This irritated Korach, Sullivan, and Dudley. So, on August 24, 2011, Dudley sent a letter to Navy League Headquarters demanding they terminate us. Mr. Daniel Branch, Jr., President of the Navy League requested Turowski and I furnish him with our documented defense as to the Dudley accusation for reasons for dismissal. It is my conjecture Dudley may have had some support at the Washington level.

We provided the documentation and details in our defense and eventually all attempts to remove us ceased. I believe there were enough Navy League cabinet members at the Washington level that knew the truth of the *Liberty* incident and aware of the injustice.

While Sullivan tried to stop us, Turowski and I have transferred our Navy League service to the Daytona Beach Navy League Council (DBNL) who welcomed us despite all of the negativity. At DBNL, Mr. Turowski continued to provide tireless support and dedication to our sailors and marines. Illegally, Sullivan sent an email to all Florida northeast area Navy League councils warning them they were to deny membership to Turowski and me. That did not stop the DBNL. I have continued to work at supporting them and satisfying my responsibilities. I am now the

USS Carney, DDG 64, liaison and I have continued my used book project. As of November 2012, I estimate 8,000 books have passed through my project and a few of the commands have sent complementary letters. In addition, as of November 2012, Sullivan, and Korach are no longer in management positions. I do not harbor any malice toward them and I wish them well. I only hope they might understand someday the grief they put Ted and I through. I tell this story not to harass them but to explain their bigotry under their oversight.

With new mangers, Washington has now backed off from dismissing us. However, Ted Turowski and I have never received an apology from anyone.

The American Legion Fiasco

The President of the USS *Liberty* Veterans Association (LVA) asked Glenn Oliphant (former Electronic Technician and *Liberty* survivor) and I to attend the American Legion (AL) Convention in Indianapolis, Minnesota, in August, 2012. Documents were sent to the LVA treasurer as a fee was to be sent to AL headquarters to enable the LVA to obtain a booth. As in previous AL conventions, we would pass out *Liberty* incident pamphlets and information from our decorated booth. Coincidently, an LVA supporter, Ted Arens, a delegate from Michigan, was planning to attend as he had a Michigan resolution to present to the AL Convention supporting a congressional investigation. Ted arrived August 22nd and made sure he would be able to present the *Liberty* resolution. AL officials confirmed Ted would speak

for five minutes. Ted then attempted to find the LVA booth and he was told there wasn't any.

On the morning of August 24th, around 8:00 AM we arrived. We went to the Indianapolis Convention center to determine the location of said booth. We asked the clerk at the check-in counter the location but she could not find our listing.

We called our LVA Treasurer and found out due to an accidental oversight, our application and fee of One Thousand Dollars were never forwarded. So, we politely asked if there was someone we could talk to in order to pay the fee and acquire the booth. At no time did Glenn or I act rude, abrasive, or demanding. The clerk made a phone call and a few minutes later, Ms. Andrea Watson arrived with two or three security guards. We told her of our plight in that I flew from Florida and Glenn drove from Centerville, Minnesota. Would she please consider giving us a booth? We were ready to charge the fee on our credit card. We could not imagine there could be a problem.

She would not have any of this as she was not there to negotiate. She told us they were there to escort us off of the premises. We pleaded with them. They were very rude and abrasive. We could not believe their attitude. At no time did Glenn or I raise our voice or demand anything from them. Their heels were dug in and that was that. They became impatient and Glenn and I left. I must mention that Glenn, a long time American Legion member, was distraught at their actions and knew they were not doing the right thing

to us. His American spirit was frustrated and he terminated his AL membership by flicking his membership card at Ms. Watson and that got Glenn in trouble. They considered this bad behavior and we were trouble makers.

On August 23rd, Ted Arens went to AL security. Wearing his *Liberty* ball cap, he found Dick Holmes. Seeing the ball cap, Mr. Holmes immediately and provocatively said to Ted, "I am sick of you bastards and I am going to throw you out on your ass". Ted replied, "Hold on—I am a delegate from Michigan representing Legionnaires advocating my resolution; get out of my face." As Ted walked away, they had more words. Ted was angry and immediately walked over to Legion headquarters where he found Judge Advocate Phil Onderdonk. Ted introduced himself and asked Onderdonk what he knew. The next words out of his mouth were unbelievable, "The ship should never have been there—it was a spy ship". He also said "Your resolution is going nowhere". The FIX was in.

⌐

The following is reported by Ted Arens.

"I always thought that the word judge implied impartiality and a person who would look at things fairly, but that was not the case. It became very apparent that many phone calls had been made to the Michigan AL headquarters regarding the resolution before I ever got

to Indianapolis. Never mind that the entire resolution was approved at the State AL convention in Kalamazoo, MI. Democracy does not exist if national headquarters does not want it. You would think that the AL would realize that there is no greater gift one can give then to give his/her life for their country. The executive leadership of the AL is so blinded by their own power trip that they no longer understand the sacred obligation they have in defending that gift. Onderdonk and Holmes had absolutely zero sympathy for the crew of the Liberty. The fact that the ship was a sitting duck, had over 3000 rounds of cannon fired at them, napalm and phosphorous and then a torpedo that blew men to hell and then purposely left abandoned for eighteen hours (so it would sink) with thirty-four dead and 174 wounded and one doctor aboard —made no difference to Holmes and Onderdonk. I wonder what kind of battles they were in—if any. The USS Liberty is the most decorated ship in Naval history for a single engagement, or perhaps ever? Strange, several years ago I was told that the ship was not even on the Navy's Vessel Registration website. It took a half a year for me to get the Liberty back on the website — I had to shame the Navy into it. They have tried to cover it up for a long time."

On August 25th the following was reported by Ted Arens:

"In discussions with many Legion members they already told me that the fix was in before I ever went to the meeting—I would not be allowed to speak. Lo and behold they were right. I went to the committee meeting on foreign

affairs and when the American resolution came up I raised my hands and said I wanted to speak. They said I could not. I said that I was a delegate from Michigan assigned to the foreign policy committee. They said my name was not on the list even though Pat Lafferty and I personally went down, talked to Joe Socci—went over to the secretary and saw her enter my name in the computer. The judge advocate had the paperwork changed."

Calendar Year 2011

My shipmate Glenn Oliphant was joined by USS *Liberty* supporter Ms. Alison Weir to operate a booth at the American Legion (AL) 2011 Convention. Everything went well until someone engaged Ms. Weir in a conversation regarding the plight of Palestinians. Ms. Weir is very informed and told the individual what she knew indicating the negative and brutal treatment of Israelis toward Palestinians. The individual did not like her honest comments and complained to AL security. Solely based on conversation, they then escorted Ms. Weir off and out of the AL convention and told her she was not welcomed ever. Glenn remained at the USS *Liberty* booth and continued his normal business of passing out information and answering questions from passing AL members with no problems or issues from AL security.

This brings me to calendar year 2013 and the American Legion sent the following letter indicating that the USS *Liberty* Veterans Association was not welcome at the 2013 American Legion convention. The letter, dated April 10, 2013, reads and I quote:

Dear Mr. Shafer (USS Liberty Veterans Association Treasurer)

On April 8, 2013, The American Legion received your application and check for a booth in the exhibit hall at the upcoming American Legion Convention in Houston, Texas, August 23-27, 2013.

Based upon your organization's actions in the last two years, we decline to have your organization participate.

Returned herewith is your application and check.

Very truly yours,
James E. Koutz
National Commander

Cc: Daneil S. Wheeler, National Adjutant
    P.B. Onderdonk, Jr., National Judge Advocate
    Convention Division

Furthermore

Based on the above American Legion action to keep the LVA from participating the 2013 convention, Ted Arens took out a AL convention Program advertisement which said the following:

USS *LIBERTY*—A CAUSE FOR JUSTICE

On June 8, 1967 the USS *Liberty* was attacked by the State of Israel resulting in the deaths of 34 Americans and the wounding of 173 out of a crew of 294. After the attack a cover up resulted through controlled and manipulated investigations by the US government. The eyewitnesses aboard the ship were not allowed to testify as to what occurred that day. Many other witnesses have come forward since, including Air Force intelligence officers, who overheard the Israeli attack jet communications identifying the ship as American.

The Navy JAG officer who investigated the USS *Liberty* attack (for only 1 week) has signed an affidavit stating that the investigation was a sham see http://www.the*liberty*incident.com/docs/boston-comments.pdf). A few courageous, highly decorated leaders have spoken out like Admiral Moorer (*Distinguished Flying Cross and 7th Chairman of the Joint Chiefs*), General Davis (*Medal of Honor*),

and Admiral Staring (*Former Judge Advocate of the Navy*) and they formed the independent "Moorer Commission" (see http://www.uss*liberty*inquiry.com/evidence/usreports/moorer.html)and judged that the attack was deliberate and that the men aboard the USS *Liberty* were murdered. During the attack the order was given to prepare to abandon ship and life rafts were lowered in the water. The life rafts were raked by machine gun fire from Israeli torpedo boats and machine gun fire was directed at *Liberty* firefighters and stretcher-bearers aiding the wounded. This action by the torpedo boat crews is an International War Crime. The men of the USS *Liberty* have filed a war crime report on June 8, 2005 as per Department of Defense Directive #5810.01B as required with the Secretary of the Army. The report has been ignored and languishes there with the Secretary.

Master Sergeant Bryce Lockwood USMC—"*My Country deserted me*".

Captain Richard Kiepfer USN—"*Never before in the history of the US Navy has a Navy board of inquiry ignored the testimony of American eyewitnesses and taken, on faith, the word of their attackers*"

THE AMERICAN LEGION NEEDS TO SUPPORT THESE MEN—Ted Arens, Post 10 Manistee, MI

On May 9, 2013, Ted Arens sent a letter to the American Legion hierarchy, indicating that he was told by Phil Onderdonk, National Judge Advocate, that Ted's check for $1,150 was being returned denying the add from appearing in the Convention Program.

Note: Apparently the American Legion had decided not to have anything to do with the plight of the *Liberty* crew. It was more important **no negative Israeli** documents or discussion occur at the 2012 convention, 2013, or future conventions rather than support a fellow veterans group.

I truly believe the American Legion is a creditable organization working hard to help veterans. However, the few that have control of their security are obviously Israeli supporters and will not tolerate anything negative toward them. It is evident that the *Liberty* crew is seen as unwanted subversive malcontents. This is a clear case of bigotry. They have done a terrible disservice to the American Legion.

Chapter 8

The Silver Lining

This chapter is dedicated to the people who have indicated to me through their actions the nature of the heart—their love for the United States as given to us from our founding fathers. These folks have stood by me or the USS *Liberty* crew in the face of adversity and condemnation. While suffering through the *Liberty* attack, deceit, frustration, persecution, and bigotry, the silver lining to this story are the people I had the honor and privilege to encounter. I hope you will find solace to know there are American patriots out there who joined our fight against *Liberty* injustice—by doing so, they risk being placed on the list by some people as anti-Semite, un-American, and sometimes they suffered financial loss.

I could not start this list without first citing the active crew of the USS *Liberty* Veterans Association (LVA). My fellow shipmates not only distinguished themselves during the attack, but also, afterwards. The LVA realized the importance of the story to America and made extreme efforts to fight for the truth. Please remember their bravery and professionalism resulted in military commendations making the USS *Liberty* the most decorated Navy ship for a single engagement. Ironically, it included the Presidential Unit

Citation from President Johnson. The inspiration shared between the crew defines the Navy spirit to "never give up the ship" and we will "never quit striving for truth". I cannot be more emphatic how much I admire and respect my fellow *Liberty* crew.

The Washington Music Store

Another casualty of the attack was the loss of my accordion. The skipper liked Sunday afternoon barbeque on the rear deck where it is large and flat. Included in the festivities were my fellow shipmates who were excellent vocalists and musicians. This was the age of "do-whop". I provided the Lawrence Welk contingent. Unfortunately, my squeeze box was in the area flooded by the torpedo. It was a total loss and the Navy provided me with a modest compensation. Upon arriving in Suitland, Maryland, my next duty station (Cheltenham Communications Station), I found a music store that sold used accordions in Washington, DC. I found a replacement; however, they were asking more than my modest compensation. My finances at the time could not afford spending anymore than the Navy funds. After playing the box, the salesman asked me if I had another accordion to trade in. When I explained what happened to it, he immediately went to the owner of the music store. I could see the embarrassment as his faced turned bright red. The owner came to us and said, "You can purchase the accordion at your price as this was the least I can do to apologize for my peoples' attack on our ship". If I felt any Jewish bigotry then, that incident wiped it out. The price I paid was substantially less than what they were asking. He made my day and I still have the accordion.

The Veterans of Foreign Wars

The VFW has faithfully supported us over the years. Each year, they publish "Support Today's Veterans & Military Priority Goals". The pamphlet is created primarily for Congress and the membership so they all know their year-to-year goals. For a number of years, the pamphlet included "Investigate the 1967 Israeli attack on the USS *Liberty*" under Defense and Foreign Affairs. The *Liberty* focus comes from its members who vote on the aforementioned goals. In other words, the VFW wants Congress to take on their cited requirements. While there are likely some Israeli supporters, nevertheless, the membership votes have determined their collective action and they respond accordingly. Unlike the American Legion, I am very proud to be a VFW member.

The Daytona Beach Council of the United States Navy League

As mentioned in chapter seven, the Daytona Beach Navy League Council (DBNL) accepted Ted Turowski and me because we were thrown out of the St. Augustine Navy League and we wanted to continue our service. The collective leadership of this council was exemplary in the way they handled the situation. That is, they objectively listened to what our intentions were. They let Ted and I provide the kind of service we are used to giving in support our sailors and marines. All the while, the area president, Bill Dudley and the northeast president, Dave Sullivan, were trying

their best to prevent us from continuing our Navy League membership. DBNL held fast and took a lot of heat from them. They restored my faith in the Navy League which was created by Teddy Roosevelt.

Richard "Dick" Thompson

I have come to love Dick Thompson as an older brother. We first met at our 22nd or 23rd LVA reunion in Washington, DC. As he walked in the door, I welcomed him and asked what I could do for him as he was not a recognized face. He told me he heard about the reunion and wanted to meet the Liberty crew. He never forgot this encounter and over the years, Dick and his family welcomed Patricia and me into their hearts. Dick retired from the Navy as a Commander; however, the function he performed in the Navy required him to wear civilian clothes. In fact, he had to borrow a uniform for his retirement ceremony. He was a decorated sailor who served with distinction in the Korean War receiving two purple hearts. We both were retired and we both lived in Florida. Dick was a happy-go-lucky guy, aggressive in business, and always proud of his family. His wife Jean is a gracious and a loving person. It was easy for us to love her too.

Dick enjoyed telling me how he came to know and support the LVA. Following the Navy, Dick became a successful 3M Sales Vice President and then Dictaphone Vice President of Sales Development.

The point is he was well traveled and met foreign dignitaries. On one such trip, he was in Beirut, Lebanon, on June 8, 1967 and planned to meet a friend socially, the CIA

station chief, William Buckley, for drinks that evening. At their encounter, Buckley told Dick he had bad news; the Israelis deliberately attacked the USS *Liberty* and suffered massive casualties. When Dick returned to his room upset by the information, he made a notation in his diary. Sadly, shortly after this meeting, William Buckley was taken hostage and killed by militant Islamics. Years later when Dick was going through his old papers and diaries with his son, a diary fell open to the above *Liberty* entry. Dick told me he then had a mental rush and the strongest desire to determine what happened to the crew and the ship—the more he learned, the more his American spirit was aroused and felt challenged to help. The crew deserved justice and the American public needed to learn the truth. Dick became totally committed.

Upon finding out that I was a CIA retiree, he found comfort in our friendship and it grew from there. While I lived in Dunn Loring, Virginia, at the time, Dick would visit from Florida and was my guest. There were times though, we did not agree about politics. Dick, if you are looking down on us, I have come to know you were right and I was hopelessly wrong. Yes, the Republican Party, as much as I appreciate what they fundamentally stand for, are hijacked by neo-conservatives. Later, when I moved to Florida, Dick came to treat Patricia and me as family and we would visit Dick and his wife, Jeannie, often. They are wonderful people and will always have a place in our hearts.

While I was still in Virginia, Dick went to Europe to get a movie produced about the *Liberty* resulting in the BBC

movie, "Dead in the Water". He told me he even went to Hollywood and talked with Clint Eastwood and others and they either never returned his call or, as in one case, had him escorted out of the building. Dick was relentless and was convinced there was a connection between the United States and Israel with regards to Israeli war plans. America had to know. As it turns out, he was right. Veteran British BBC investigative reporter, Peter Haunen, went to Israel and filmed discussions with the Israeli war planners. Peter also wrote a book called, "Operation Cyanide" with additional details Dick and Peter uncovered. Unfortunately, the book is currently out of print. The BBC movie is currently available as Dick gave me the copyrights to the movie in trust for the LVA. Since his demise, the movie is reaching more and more people. The BBC, Peter Hounen, and Mr. Thompson have made an important and valuable mark in American history.

I also want to mention that Mr. Thompson was initially in the Navy Underwater Demolition Team (UDT) and a submariner. As a navy scuba diver in the early fifties, the underwater equipment they used was not perfected. Every dive was a challenge and dangerous. In addition, during the Korean Conflict, he was utilized as a target spotter. That is, the submarine would put Dick in the water to swim ashore without being detected by the enemy and then he would call in artillery. He earned two purple hearts in this manner.

Dick also developed a friendship with a Russian submarine Admiral Nikolai Cherkoschin. He made trips

to Russia after the Soviet Union fell and the Russian submariner accepted Dick as an old friend and fellow submariner. He told Dick America and Soviets came close to a nuclear war during the June 67 war. He said they dispatched forty Soviet submarines off the east coast of America. Meanwhile, the Admiral was a Captain on a submarine stationed near Haifa. His orders were to use his nuclear tipped cruse missile to destroy Haifa if Israel invaded Cairo and/or Damascus as they were their client states. Dick had the Admiral's testimony taped and added to the BBC movie, "Dead in the Water". Dick had discovered how concerned and serious the Soviets considered this war.

Dick died driving back from Mclean, Virginia, after spending four days with us during the LVA's fortieth year reunion, June 10. 2007. He was seventy-seven. Witnesses to the accident said his brake lights never came on and he was traveling about seventy miles an hour when he hit a tree. We believe he passed out possibly from a seizure or medications. His death was very hard to take personally. His family asked me to give his eulogy. Difficult as it was, I could not say enough then and now of how much of an American patriot Dick Thompson was and how much I miss him. His legacy lives on as he has become my inspiration to never give up this fight for the truth.

Colonel William Barrett Taylor III, USAF, (Ret.)

I met Col. Taylor through Dick Thompson and a friendship ensued. He started out in the Army Air Corps during WWII flying B-24 Liberators but eventually became an Air

Force lawyer. He had a passion for the Air Force retiring in 1964. On a trip to Washington, Barrett had me drive to the Air Force monument. He told me he was asked to critique its preliminary design and told them he hated it. Every time he encountered it, he would become agitated.

Barrett was instrumental in obtaining legislation to create the Air Force academy and he served as its first deputy. After retirement, he became very involved in the Republican Party assisting President Nixon's election who then appointed Col. Taylor in 1969 to Senior U.S. Commissioner to the South Pacific Commission (a group of small Island countries of the Pacific Basin). He served there for five years. His service to the country and industry was far and wide. He also worked for Douglas Aircraft on their international sales staff retiring in 1975.

Col. Taylor's passion to guide the United States down the right plane shifted to helping the *Liberty*. Barrett was a determined *Liberty* supporter and tried everything he could think about to obtain justice for the crew. I had the pleasure of going to his house in Tampa, Florida, for a planning session and stayed at his house in Arlington, Virginia. He was a friend and down to earth as they come. I was amazed of past and present American officials including Senator John Warner that Barrett called friends. Along with Rear Admiral Merlin Staring, USN (Ret.), he challenged Senator Warner who was chairman of the Senate Arms Services Committee to look into the *Liberty* issue. While nothing came of it, it was the closet we came to getting a congressional investigation. Barrett could not do enough for us.

He passed away on March 21, 2008. The LVA will miss his guidance but more importantly his friendship.

Note: In order to obtain specifically what motivated the following individuals, I asked them the following question and they provided their answers: "What is it about the USS Liberty event that influenced your American spirit"?

Richard Thompson, Jr.

Reply: My answer is two fold:

1. *Your friendship, and I include Patricia too, is most appreciated and we are so grateful for you guys. We love you both so much. I speak for my Mom and my whole family. My Dad loved you so and had the utmost respect and passion for the USS Liberty crew and their journey through this most despicable cover up and black eye to all who ever swore allegiance to America and served with distinction. The story of the USS Liberty, your story, is just a crying shame on our republic. Most Americans still don't know the story of the USS Liberty. You asked me to speak about how the USS Liberty changed my life. And how the story changed my perspective of America. Well, let me just say...in many ways it shattered my American Dream. I was the oldest of 6 children and grew up in Alexandria, Virginia. My Dad was a successful 3M Sales VP, and also VP of Sales development and Dictaphone. My Mom was a home maker. We went*

to St Mary's, the Catholic School, Grades K-8. Our beautiful neighborhood off the Potomac, directly across the river from Ft Washington, was Waynewood. There we honed the American dream —a solid Middle Class family. We took a week or two vacation every summer, we were aware my Dad worked very hard as bread winner, and my Mom stayed 100% engaged as a dedicated Mom. We eventually moved to Florida as my Dad's career required more extensive travel to Europe and even the Middle East. I'm not sure exactly when my Dad and I had serious conversations about the USS Liberty. But once he told me the story, I looked at him eyeball to eyeball and said.., "No Way...that can be true"...Because I had the most respect for his knowledge and patriotism, I couldn't believe my ears. But NEVER, would our country leave our Military behind in the cowardly way he described! And President Johnson giving direct orders???? No Way! Those were my thoughts...and that is what I communicated to Dad. No Way! You (Dad) have missed some pieces to this puzzle.

Israel's attack on the ship was cowardly and Israel had the audacity to do it since the Liberty had only four 50 caliber machine gun was nothing to what the Israelis had in their arsenal. On other words, the Liberty was "duck in the pond" to the Israeli gunners.

Richard Thompson, Jr. is the son of Dick Thompson mentioned above. My relationship with Rich is an extension

of the loving relationship developed between our families. As with the others, Rich's support for the *Liberty* has been steadfast. He has said to me the *Liberty* story has opened his eyes and given serious thought about this travesty on Capital Hill not investigating the attack.

Ted Turowski

> *1. Reply: No American ship should be attacked by any nation (friend or foe) without reprisals.*

Ted Turowski is a retired Navy Chief you want watching your back in battle. I am proud to call him "my friend". His dedication to America is unwavering. We met attending the St. Augustine Navy League Council (SANL) meeting. Living in the same neighborhood, starting in 2006, Ted and I would take turns driving to the St. Johns Library for the meetings. While not knowing anything about the Navy League, Ted became my mentor prodding me to eventually take on the liaison to the USS Farragot. He then became the President of the SANL, 2008 to 2010, at which I excelled in my duties and responsibilities. Ted was always there to help and counsel me and we became very good friends. I know of no other Navy Leaguer who comes close to Ted's hard work and determination to help our sailors and marines. He continually created avenues for the Sea Cadets and the Navy League members to achieve both Navy and Coast Guard experiences. He planned both large and small events at Kings Bay Submarine Base, Mayport Naval Station, and Mayport Coast Guard facility. Ted is currently the liaison to a cruiser, the USS Gettysburg, CG 64.

As indicated in chapter Eight, all hell broke loose when William Korach took over SANL presidency. Ted was tenacious to ensure this wrong was turned around. The more he pushed, the more Dudley, Sullivan, and Korach pushed back. They did not appreciate this chief telling them they were amiss. At the infamous April 2010 meeting when I was terminated, Ted rose from his chair and really dressed them down. That was used to eventually cause Ted to leave SANL. At the time, Mr. Turowski was a Navy League Director and assisting the Daytona Beach Navy League Council (DBNL). Once Dudley and Sullivan realized that Ted moved on to DBNL and I had joined Ted, they took action to warn the council we were not welcomed in the Navy League any longer. Since we did not leave and DBNL ignored their advice, they then tried to have the Washington office terminate our membership. That infuriated Ted further—all the while supporting me and the USS *Liberty* cause.

My friendship with Ted has cost him both in aggravation and his pocket. The round trip to Mayport Naval Station is 150 miles and he made numerous trips helping me deliver books. Driving a large SUV, cost him exceedingly as we made three to four trips a month. Every time we made the trip, it would also take him away from his real estate business. During the one and one half hour drive each way, we would get into political discussions and we did not agree all the time. There were times we would deliberately antagonize the other just to stimulate conversation. The drive would pass quickly and we both enjoyed the camaraderie. In my eyes, Ted passes the test of an honorary Liberty crew. Yes, I would go into battle

with Ted anytime and take a bullet for him if necessary.

Ted Arens

Reply: We should honor the sons and daughters in the Armed Services especially those who gave their life. I think it is treachery some politicians abrogate their duties and responsibilities and hide behind their desks to protect their political behinds.

Ted Arens, a former Marine, has been a solid *Liberty* supporter. As indicated in chapter seven, Ted encountered and interacted with the legal and security staff of the American Legion Convention in August 2012 and 2013. In addition, he has written numerous letters to Congressmen including the President and successfully campaigned within the Michigan American Legion.

He was born on September 23, 1947 in Groesbeek, the Netherlands. The reason for his passion derives as an immigrant to the United States in 1959. Ted enlisted in the Marines in 1967 and saw action in the De-militarized Zone in Vietnam. With the GI Bill in hand, he obtained an electrical engineering degree and eventually established a successful machining tool controls company, Stegner Electric Controls in 1978. He sold the company in 2003. Mr. Arens has told me many times how grateful he is. He knows what the country has allowed him to accomplish and consequently loves this country deeply. He has set up three veteran endowments in Manistee, Mason, and Cadillac counties in Michigan with his partner George Wagoner.

He believes that politicians and military leaders have an obligation and duty to stand up for those who have made the ultimate sacrifice for America. Yet these people choose to protect their careers first.

He understands the wrong committed by Congress, the Navy, and others. He wants justice for the *Liberty* crew. If not corrected, this negative legacy will corrupt our Middle East politics and the United States Navy. Ted also provided major financial donations to the LVA. He also is committed to see justice for the crew. In my eyes, Ted passes the test of an honorary *Liberty* crew. Yes, I would go into battle with Ted anytime also.

North Palm

> *Reply: Over the years you listen to our so called "public servants," our elected "leaders" and you come to realize how they outright lie and distort facts, anything to stay in power, it becomes quite clear that their number one priority is money and power, their own well being. They grovel before Mammon, they sold their souls to the Anti Christ. No matter what the Zionist Lobby demands plus ninety percent including our politicians hand it to them on a silver platter, no questions asked. They sold out to a foreign element for Thirty Silver Shekels; they are TRAITORS in no uncertain terms. And they have no shame The only hope for this country since the lumpen masses are too distracted by their Bread and Circuses, twittering and twattering on their I-Phones,*

cell phones and the intern et facebook, the only hope is for a Coup d' Etta by the Military. They should take over the government, arrest, put on trial, imprison and hang the worst offenders from the highest lamp posts in D.C. [District of Corruption]. After cleaning house for a two or three year period, it should then be mandated that we have minimum four or five political parties allowed to run for office, lobbyists will be outlawed and corporate donations will be outlawed. Three or four months before the elections, all contenders will have equal time/ exposure in the media, radio, T.V., and newspapers at the expense of the media. As it stands now, we no longer live in a democracy but a Plutocracy. As it stands now, this is the beginning of the end for what used to be the greatest country in the world.   Pax Vobiscum

When I learned about the Liberty, I was really upset and angry that our so called leaders were actually bought and paid for TRAITORS. That is what got me started.

I met North Palm (as he wants to be identified) after contacting me about expanding his USS *Liberty* advertising. I discovered that North Palm, a committed Navy supporter, had been taking out small but potent advertisements in newspapers across the country since 2002. He had become so upset and concerned determined this was and is the best course of action to bring attention to the *Liberty* attack. This advertisement idea has spread the word about the *Liberty* incident across America. His advertisement

reads, "Duplicity, Treason, and Murder – check out: www. uss*liberty*.org." His advertisement, small two column by two inch ad would appeared in thirteen newspapers over a period of couple of months costing him thousands of dollars. He never asked for financial reimbursement as he felt a calling to spread the word of the *Liberty*'s injustice. He also had business card size cards (with the above printed on the card) made. North Palm would leave them in doctors' offices, library books, and on college bulletin boards. He also places them in junk mail with pre-paid envelops. Internationally, twice a year, June and November, he spreads the word in Germany, Austria, and Switzerland. In addition, he mails 500 to 700 newspapers to Veterans Organizations around the U.S.

North Palm joined the Navy in 1949. Following boot camp, he was assigned to the USS Leyte CV-32 for two years and saw action in the Korean Conflict. His next assignment was the USS Gilbert Islands, CVE-107. With his four years behind him, he continued to provide patriotic activity by sponsoring foreign Navy Officers at the U.S. Navy War College, Newport, R.I. for many years. With the above in mind, he objectively came to realize the crew of the *Liberty* needed his help and by God, he was going to do something. The Lord has been very generous to provide folks like North Palm the inspiration and understanding to ignite that spiritual fire becoming an activist.

Rich Siegel

Reply: While Mr. Siegel did not specifically answer my question, he provided the following prayer which I believe is very beautiful and spiritually moving.

My Prayer

I recognize that there is One God, One Love, everywhere present, that the fabric of the Universe is made of this One Love, One Spirit, that The One expresses as star, as rock, as sand, as tree, as flower, as bird, as snail, as fish, as mammal, as all of matter, and all of life from the lowest to the highest, that this One Love expresses as Humanity in all its races and cultures, and that all of Humankind's religions are attempts to embrace and access the One Love which is our truest, deepest, eternal nature; are attempts to KNOW our eternal nature, and to unite with our source, One God, One Love.

I know, that as God expresses as Me, that God and I are One. I know equally that as God expresses as my brothers and sisters, that I am One with all my brothers and sisters, and that my brothers and sisters are all One with God. I know that the three Abrahamic faiths all teach that there is One God, and so I know that I am one with all Muslims and Christians and Jews. I also know that I am one with all peoples of all faiths around the world and one with people who do not acknowledge faith. I am unified

in Spirit with all of God's human family. That spirit is made of Love and it thrives in an environment of peace. I embrace all of my human family, and all of the planet, with all its life forms, in the spirit of peace.

I affirm that the spirit of peace lives and thrives in the Holy Land. I affirm that all its children grow up in an atmosphere of peace, justice, equality, abundance, nurturing, and good will. I affirm, as it is written, Lo Yisa Goy El Goy Cherev, V'lo Yilm' Du Od Milchama. Nation Shall Not Lift Up Sword Against Nation, Neither Shall They Know War Any More.

I deny that old and antiquated ways of thinking have any power any more. I deny that any association of religion with ideas of bigotry, tribal chauvinism, or preferential relationship with God, have any sway over the followers of the three Abrahamic faiths any more. I deny that true followers of the One God, will ever misinterpret the will of God in such a way that they use it to harm their fellow man, any more. I deny that selfish economic motive can have any more power in a spiritually evolving humanity.

I re-affirm that the followers of the three Abrahamic faiths, and all faiths, and those that do not follow a faith, live in accordance with their awareness of all humankind as brethren. I see swords being turned into plowshares in the Holy Land, and all over the planet. I see America shutting down all

of its overseas bases and bringing all of its troop's home. I see the dismantling of all nuclear warheads, beginning in a place called Dimona. I see my Jewish people re-interpreting our history, taking responsibility for it, ceasing to consider "What's good for the Jews," and instead considering "What's good for all humankind," knowing that what's good for all is what's good for the Jews. I see the end of Jewish supremacy in the Holy Land, and I see those who have been cast out invited to return to conditions of peace and brotherhood. I see Jews humbly surrendering properties that have been stolen to those who lost them.

I see the followers of the three Abrahamic faiths removing any and all notions of bigotry from their religious teachings. I see the end to all bigotry against ethnic and religious groups, the end to all bigotry against women, the end to all bigotry against homosexuals. I see the end to all un-evolved notions of God, as a man with a beard and a book, sitting on a cloud, having any dealing with favorite tribes or people or real estate. I see the end to the concept of "chosen-ness," and I see all peoples aware that all are equally chosen.

I see myself bringing my family to enjoy Gaza as a peaceful beach resort, with no threat of IDF bombs. I see myself harvesting olives in the West Bank, with my Palestinian brothers and sisters, under conditions of peace, with no threat of settler violence. I see

*myself traveling the Holy Land, north to south, east
to west, being equally welcomed in mosque, syna-
gogue, and church. I see the teachings of Mohammed,
of Jesus, and of the Jewish prophets, respected by all.
I see the joy of peaceful co-existence, of diversity, and
the awareness of unity in that diversity.*

*I see all these things because I know that all my
human brothers and sisters are infinitely capable
of knowing their oneness with God, and with each
other, and are infinitely capable of taking on their
first and most important responsibility: to care for
the angels that God gives us to care for: our children
and our neighbors' children.*

*I release this prayer to God and God's Universe, as
I see the gentle hush of peace in the Holy Land and
all over the planet, as I lay myself to sleep with the
joyful expectation that the morning will bring the
sounds of the playful laughter of all the children of
the planet, living in peace.*

And I am grateful.
And so it is.
Amen.
Rich Siegel

Rich Siegel was introduced to me during my New York—
Connecticut speaking tour. Rich, a song writer, singer, and
pianist par excellence impressed me both as a Liberty supporter and Jew. That is, the current plight of Palestinians at
the hands of a belligerent Israeli government stresses Mr.

Siegel and has created an album of songs called, "The Way to Peace". He cares for all people and with that said, he has written the aforementioned prayer. The prayer is an inspiration to us all.

Doctor Robert Kamansky, DDS, Ret.

Reply: I am a proud Jew whose family emigrated from Russia seeking liberty. I have found Israel's deliberate attack on the USS Liberty broke the Ten Commandments which I hold dear and threatens my liberty. The Liberty crew are veterans and they need justice and I feel compelled to give back and help them.

Doctor Kamansky and I became acquainted at a Washington, DC membership meeting and a series of events for the American Cold War Veterans which included a memorial service at Arlington Cemetery. At first, Doctor Kamansky who is Jewish was unsure about my explanation of the USS *Liberty* story because he remembers Rabbis telling their flocks Israel could not deliberately attack an American navy ship. However, over time, not only did he believe my version, but went to extremes to acquire details and proof spending hours sifting through documents. He made numerous trips to Washington, DC and the Nixon Library located not far from his home reviewing tons of recently de-classified material. He was aided by Doctor Patrick Pacalo and my shipmate Donald Pageler (former CT). Doctor Bob was instrumental in helping Doctor Pacalo write his book on the *Liberty*. Doctor Bob, as I like to call

him, also has been very generous by providing funds to establish the USS *Liberty* welfare foundation. His support of the USS *Liberty* crew has been steadfast and extremely vigorous. He has opened many doors. When given a hint of political conspiracy, he has been tenacious to acquire evidence and truth. I am proud to call him my friend. Indeed America has developed patriotic sons because of our values.

Doctor Patrick J. Pacalo, Phd., CPT (AUS), CP

> *Reply: You might add that I first learned of the USS Liberty when I was reading one of my Dad's Naval Institute Proceedings magazines in the later 1970s. The magazine had a review of Ennes' book and gave the basics of the story, taking no position. (My Dad is a retired Naval Aviator). Since reading that review, I always wondered what had happened there, and that is why when you introduced yourself as a member of the Liberty Survivors I was very interested. This is no reflection on me (what I am about to say), but rather a reflection on the compelling story, that when The Liberty Cipher came out I sent a copy to "Wings of Gold," the magazine of the US Naval Aviation Association—they ran a very brief story and did NOT dismiss the book as some kind of crack-pot story. Judging from this and other things I have heard a number of highly placed Navy vets wonder what happened. As well I gave copies of the book to several of my friends that are Vietnam (Army) veterans, and they were very intrigued by the story*

and told others. There might be more people out
there than we know who are interested in the story
of the Liberty and why it happened.

I met Doctor Pacalo, a doctor of History, through Doctor
Kamansky. He also is a member of the American Cold War
Veterans (ACWV). He authored "The *Liberty* Cipher, Cold
Warfare IV". He acquired de-classified material from the
National Security Achieve center and the National Secu-
rity Agency at Fort Meade, Maryland. His support for the
ACWV stems from the many military personnel who were
killed or injured fighting the "Cold War". Pat was an Army
Captain paratrooper becoming seriously injured on a jump.

He enthusiastically embraced the *Liberty* story. It was
obvious his investigative curiosity of historical events fire
was ignited. With the guidance and assistance of Doctor
Kamansky, Doctor Pat dove into mountains of *Liberty* data
to develop his interesting book. It is indeed worth the read.
A copy of "*Liberty* Cipher" was accepted, approved, and can
be found in the prestigious Army-Navy Club Library in
Washington, DC. In addition, Doctor Pat has written four
other books that I am aware.

Alison Weir

Reply: The USS Liberty story moves me in so many
intensely emotional ways:

- *Meeting the survivors is a powerful experience:*
  hearing these men describe the carnage, the
  excruciating pain, the terror, the tragedy...

- *Hearing sisters describe beloved brothers who were killed, wives describe lost husbands, sons talk of fathers who were taken from them, mothers remember cherished gone-forever sons...*
- *The shunting aside of these men and of their families by the military establishment, the US government, the media, is intolerable...*
- *The enormity of the cover-up... the lies, the smears against the victims and their supporters, the continuing carnage against men, women, and children in the Middle East enabled by burying the facts on the USS Liberty...*
- *The fact that other young men, and now young women, are being sent to fight unnecessary wars on behalf of a foreign country that killed their predecessors and in a military that abandoned the men attacked by this cruel and false ally....*
- *The determination not to allow these men and their families to be forgotten; to bring justice, honesty, truth, and in so doing to help to finally end the continuing massacres and cruelty and devastation and destruction of young lives in Palestine and throughout the Middle East; to stop the corruption of our own country, to end the peril engulfing our children, to stop the rot...*
- *To work toward an honorable, shining, strong, safe country for my grandchildren... and for a world in which everyone's grandchildren are safe, happy, and at peace.*
- *I'm the founder and executive director of "If*

*Americans Knew," a nonpartisan organization
to give Americans the facts on Israel-Palestine,
and president of the Council for the National
Interest, founded by former Congressional representatives and Foreign Service officers to work
toward Middle East policies based on American
principles and interests... I grew up in a military
family and was born at West Point while my
father was a tactical officer there; my father was
an Air Force officer and three of my uncles were
career Army, Air Force, and Naval officers...*

Alison, Don Pageler, and I worked a booth at an American Legion Convention at Phoenix, AR. Her command
of details regarding the *Liberty* attack was so daunting
she could have been a survivor herself. I have never met
a woman who is so committed to see the Palestinians and
others affected by Israel's belligerency peacefully resolved.
She is tireless in her commitment. While Middle East justice is primary, justice for the *Liberty* crew is another goal
included in her portfolio and we are truly thankful for that.

Alison Weir is the executive director of "If Americans
Knew". She founded this independent investigation as
a freelance journalist in 2001. The focus was the West
Bank and Gaza which were rarely visited by American
reporters. She is also the President of the Council for the
National Interest which seeks to encourage and promote
a U.S. foreign policy in the Middle East that is consistent
with American values, protects or national interests, and
contributes to a just solution of the Arab-Israeli conflict.

With those aims and attributes, I am very proud to call this woman activist my friend. Thank God our country produces citizens of her caliber and we could use a lot more of them.

Chas Folcik

> *Reply: After learning that Ernie and Ted Turwoski wanted to relocate their Navy League membership to our council, I was erroneously advised by Dave Sullivan and supported by Bill Dudley (Northeast and all Florida presidents respectively) to deny them the transfer from the St. Augustine council. After checking with national if Sullivan and Dudley had the authority, I was informed they did not. Therefore, knowing about the Liberty attack and cover up, I was emboldened to stand up for Ernie and Ted and allow them to join our council as they were unfairly handled as Dudley and Sullivan tried to railroad them out of the Navy League. I was not going to let that happen as president of the Daytona Beach Council of the U. S. Navy League.*

Ray Huther

> *Reply: Ernie Gallo rekindled the USS Liberty attack in my mind. I admit that I was not aware of the things he experienced and about which he has written and spoken. As such they will reside forever in the low spots in the history of our Navy and of our government, there certainly appears to be an*

attempt to keep the attack out of the limelight. If it is a conscious effort – it is succeeding.

The incidents Ernie writes about while a crew member on the Liberty and as a member of the Navy League are totally disgusting to say the least. Both reek of the very dark side of politics. It begins in the highest office in the land with the refusal to intervene during a vicious attack on the USS Liberty when powerful Navy resources were ordered to stand down to avoid offending an ally undertaking the killing and wounding of our brave sailors and the attempt to sink their ship.

Over four decades later ties to the attack on the Liberty have lead to Ernie's gross mistreatment at the league council level, the region level, the state level and all the way to the office of the Navy League President. My perception is that the latter may have found himself between a rock and a hard-spot with the case. Should he automatically follow the push of the council, region and state leadership (and friendships that may have been established over time) or should he give the accused a platform upon which a defense might be justly presented?

Joining Ernie with the threat of ejection from the Navy League was Ted Turowski, a fellow NL member who outwardly and without hesitation questioned how Ernie was being treated at a St Augustine BOD meeting.

Both were denied hearings of sort to hear the trumped-up charges. Ernie was even told to prove he was not a bigot. In actuality, one leveling the charge

of bigotry—the accuser—the president of the local council—should have proved the accused was a bigot and not visa versa. How is it possible to prove one is not something?

Things dragged on and on for Ernie and Ted. They were insulted and frustrated as their names were dragged through the mud throughout the state by those with the goal of removing them from their beloved Navy League of the United States. Silence was the accuser's strategy when attempts were made by the accused to clear their names. When finally the accusers seemed to give up by withdrawing their charges, their actions remained silent— no apology—no broadcasting about the innocence of two dedicated and hard working league members—nothing. The accusers maintain their strategy of silence while perceptions of guilt most likely remain throughout the Navy family.

Ernie and Ted, both of whom I have known for several years, are fine gentleman with a love for family, country and the U.S. Navy. They are two of the most active members in their "new" council in Daytona Beach. Their council assignments have set new and higher standards for the council. They excel in their service to the troops and their family members.

I am still upset over how these two patriots were treated but my love of the sea services is as strong as ever and I will continue to work for the troops and their families as do Ernie and Ted. My faith

in the Navy League though is tarnished somewhat by what I would call child-like actions and poor leadership in an attempt to destroy the reputations of two fine people while protecting their council brother exhibiting the same traits.

I met both Chas Folcik and Ray Huther at the Daytona Beach Area Council of the United States Navy League. Chas was President and Ray was Vice-President and they both welcomed Ted Turowski and me into their council even though they had been warned we were "bad apples" by the Northeast Florida Navy League President, Dave Sullivan. Since we were both active type members especially Ted, it was not long before we were given assignments. This happened while the Florida President, Bill Dudley, was communicating with the Washington, DC office attempting to sack Ted and me from the Navy League. Without knowing us from Adam, Chas and Ray not only stood their ground to keep us but they wrote complimentary letters to Washington supporting us thereby risking their tenure and reputation. I was astonished and elated with their commitment and determination to keep us as members. I thank God our country creates people like these that objectively think issues through and then act before caving to authority, otherwise Ted and I would have been Navy League history and not the productive members we currently are.

Chapter 9

The Ultimate Silver Lining & More

The response I received from Doctor Tony Wells was so impressive, remarkable, and inspiring I felt it required a separate chapter. It deserves to stand alone as he objectively provides details of the "why" the IDF deliberately attacked. I am deeply indebted to Doctor Wells for allowing me to print the following analysis.

Doctor Tony Wells, *PhD.*

> *Reply: What sparks my American spirit about LIBERTY is very simple: USS LIBERTY's crew exemplified the finest traditions of the United States Navy in combat, and the very best qualities of the American people in a war environment—courage, loyalty, determination, dedication, skill, tenacity, and personal sacrifice; added to these great qualities is the key fact that brave American sailors on board USS LIBERTY not only acted in the finest traditions of the US Navy they performed their duties above and beyond the call of duty, as was represented by the award of the Congressional Medal of Honor to the Commanding Officer. Their courage was not fully recognized*

by the government of the day and the fact that the Johnson Administration played down LIBERTY's heroic acts is to the enduring shame of that Administration. It behooves the United States to rightfully place on record the full story of what happened to the USS LIBERTY in 1967 and provide a fitting lasting memorial to all the brave men of the most highly decorated warship in the history of the United States.

Note: Doctor Wells. PhD. is a doctor of History and was assigned the White House Middle East historian in 1967. The Lord works in mysterious ways or does He have a plan. To wit: Here is another case when out of the clear blue sky; this gentleman seeks out our group to provide us with his guidance. He told me he knew exactly why the Israelis deliberately attacked the *Liberty* but could not tell us because of his secrecy oath. I fully understand and respect this limitation and his strong moral commitment. Nevertheless, his words of wisdom make a lot of sense.

SPEECH TO THE USS LIBERTY VETERANS' ASSOCIATION AT THEIR 40TH ANNIVERSARY DINNER, JUNE 10TH, 2007

It is a great honor to be with you all this evening to mark the 40th Anniversary of the attack upon the United States Ship *LIBERTY*, and to be gathered to honor the memory of those who perished, those who were injured, those who have subsequently passed on, and those survivors who can no longer be with us this evening, and finally of course the brave survivors whom we are all so proud to see united together.

I would also like to thank you all for inviting me to be your guest speaker. When I first came in touch directly with the *LIBERTY* survivors I did as one who had knowledge of events, had been involved in various analytical initiatives, and who had written about the *LIBERTY*. Now I feel like a member of the family, and one who passionately believes in and totally supports the cause that you have all been pursuing.

What I would like to do is explain how I became involved; some things that I know about and would like to share with you, and then discuss some ways ahead that I feel may be useful. The issues and causes, and I use the word causes in the legal sense, are very much relevant and dynamic today for the United States as a whole and the US Navy in particular. Why is this? Fundamentally it is about the truth, and ensuring that the record is set straight. It is about honoring the memory

of those who gave their lives for this country, and in so doing we have to go through the process of analyzing in fine detail all the events surrounding the June War of 1967. I am not so sure that we as a Nation have truly learned all the lessons from the June War, and indeed implemented them in ways that will make our Navy more capable and our Foreign Policy and global strategy more successful.

How then did Tony Wells get involved? I will work backwards. Mr. David Walsh wrote an article "Friendless Fire" in the June 2003 Edition of the US Naval Institute Proceedings. His case was compelling and accurate, though not complete in some important detail in my opinion. His article forthrightly asserted that the book, "The *Liberty* Incident: The 1967 Attack on the US Navy Spy Ship," by a retired Naval Reserve Captain, A Jay Cristol, was seriously flawed. I completely and utterly agree with Mr. Walsh's conclusion. Mr. Walsh then came in for severe criticism, not by any objective standards of scholarship or analytical rigor, let alone substantive fact, but solely because he had challenged the Cristol thesis. At this point I wrote an article for the Proceedings that some of you may have read. It both supported Mr. Walsh while seeking to add more background and detail to his main contentions. I will talk more about the substantive aspects in a moment. I then came under fire, and I think that the Proceedings found itself in the middle of a sort of literary firefight at one level, while at another level there was an almost sinister aspect. I began to get calls inviting me to have lunch to discuss matters when I knew full well that the invi-

tations were inspired by the Israeli lobby. I naturally declined. After some time the Proceedings did publish one short, but most important piece, that said very succinctly that the attack upon the *LIBERTY* was declared deliberate in their memoirs by both Dean Rusk and the CIA Director at the time. This was the last piece that I think Proceedings would entertain, but it did end that particular debate with a positive for the USS *LIBERTY*, since the Cristol lobby had tried to undermine both Mr. Walsh and myself. So how did I get to write such an article in 2003 and how may I claim a good measure of reliability? Let me explain.

In the mid 1970s the US Navy assembled a very fine team of Cold War specialists. At the unclassified level their work can be read in the book, "Soviet Naval Diplomacy" (Pergamon Press, 1979). I was a member of this team and researched and wrote the part dealing with the June 1967 Arab Israeli War. I also wrote a CNA Professional Paper number 204, dated October 1977, entitled, "The 1967 June War. Soviet Naval Diplomacy and the Sixth Fleet – A Reappraisal". I would like to take a few minutes to explain the wider context of the Israeli attack upon the LIBERTY. I had full access at the Top Secret and SCI levels and used the latest research tools for the time. In addition I conducted special interviews with late Secretary of State Dean Rusk and his key advisor Helmut Sonnenfeldt. Please note that my initial focus was Soviet. We were trying in the mid 1970s to fully understand the Soviets' modus operandi, their strategic goals, and the role that their growing naval power would play in pursuit of their national self interests.

In parallel to this I realized that a key question was what had motivated Israel to perpetrate such an egregious act against the USS *LIBERTY*? What were the total circumstances, strategic and operational, that led the Israeli leadership making the fateful decision to attack and destroy a US eavesdropping ship operating in international waters at the end of the Six-Day War—a war that witnessed Israel redefining its boundaries and asserting its military supremacy. I concluded in 1976-1977, and still believe today, that it was the strategic underpinnings and US-Soviet relations that hold the answer to these questions. What I concluded was that Israel's actions during the Six day War brought US-Soviet relations to a stressful peak not seen since the Cuban Missile Crisis. Was Israel's attack on the *LIBERTY* an act of blatant and brutal Israeli realpolitik? Let us address this assertion.

To do this let me just recap a few salient facts. In May 1967 President Nasser of Egypt took several major aggressive acts against Israel at the same time that the Syrian government began to encourage the Palestinians to intensify guerilla operations against Israel (Wells, Soviet Naval Diplomacy, P. 158). On June 5, 1967 Israel launched a stunning preemptive attack. By June 10, when a Cease-Fire was established, Israel had defeated Egypt, Jordan, and Syria, occupied the Sinai Peninsula, the West Bank of the Jordan River and had taken the Golan Heights.

Why then attack the *LIBERTY* on June 8? The Soviet Union was a key player, not in the shadows but as a demonstrative protagonist.

The Soviets were supporting the new Syrian regime to the hilt – economic and military aid, while Palestinian guerilla operations from Syrian bases against Israel were intensified. At the same time the Soviets turned up the gain in supporting Nasser in Egypt. In mid May 1967 the Syrians protested to the Soviets that the Israelis were going to invade Syria, occupy Damascus and topple the Baathist regime. I provided details of Nasser's further belligerent acts in "Soviet Naval Diplomacy". The Soviets were obstructionist, derailing international peace efforts. At this point your brave men in the *LIBERTY* were forward deployed. They were at the pointy end of the spear. In one sense, as an eavesdropping ship, they were the point of the spear. What did Washington want? The Administration wanted to be inside the mindset and intentions of all the main players, including Israel. The *LIBERTY* was on station to help unravel the plans, intentions, and operations of the key players.

Let me make one very key point—Israel's plan could spell disaster for US-Soviet relations—an attack upon Syria, Moscow's client.

Let me sidestep a little for a few moments, and then come back to the main theme. Where was the US Navy while all this was happening? The Soviet Fifth Eskadra, their Sixth Fleet equivalent for want of a better comparison, was qualitatively and quantitatively weak compared with the Sixth Fleet, despite Soviet augmentations via the Turkish Straits. However, the Soviets made their moves and created what became known later as standard anti-

carrier task groups, with the effective shadowing of the AMERICA and SARATOGA Battle groups. The word tattletale entered the US Navy's lexicon at this time. The Soviets' main thrust was to occur with its ground forces and in particular its airborne forces. Both the US and the Soviet Union showed restraint at sea, despite incidents in East Asia in the Sea of Japan on May 10 and May 11 1967. In my work in the 1970s it became very clear exactly how Moscow intended to respond militarily, and 40 years later it still sends a shiver down my spine, particularly in light of the conversations that I had with Dean Rusk.

Did the Soviet Union plan to intervene and why? The answer is "yes," the "why" is because Israel intended to invade Syria and take Damascus. This single fact is the key. In response the Soviets planned to do two things: provide military re-supply to Syria and to intervene directly. The Soviets began operations on June 8, 1967, the day that the *LIBERTY* was attacked. The Soviet plan was to launch Red Army paratroopers into Syria and place them between an advancing Israeli army and Damascus. AN-12 CUB aircraft, the standard Soviet paratroop and cargo transport, were used, flying from fields in Hungary across Yugoslavia and then over the Adriatic and Mediterranean to Syria. The Soviet operational plans and actions were not spontaneous reactions to the Israeli advance. They were well planned in advance, with Yugoslavia granting over-flight rights. The Soviets were poised to take on the Israelis. I wrote thirty years ago, "The threat to intervene was raised

again—intensively—when the Syrian forces collapsed as the Israelis stormed the Golan Heights on June 9, a collapse that left the road to Damascus virtually undefended." The Cold War balance was now becoming dangerously out of kilter. USS *LIBERTY* was a key source in the NSA network. The Hotline quickly became an extraordinary successful means of preventing a major conflict. Moscow made it clear—if the Israelis did not desist the Red Army would execute a massive airborne drop into Syria and confront the Israeli army.

In March 1977 I interviewed separately Dean Rusk and Helmut Sonnenfeldt. I became privy to unique perspectives and data not previously released. Both men gave their permission to publish their comments. Dean Rusk told me that he and President Johnson "had never assumed any other "that the Soviets would use their airborne forces. I wrote the following about Dean Rusk, "his feelings at the time were one of despair if the Cease-Fire had not held and the Israelis not halted when they did" (Wells, P. 166, Soviet naval Diplomacy). I asked Dean Rusk what the US would have done. He believed that the US would have landed Sixth Fleet aircraft in Israel to deter the Soviets from invading Israel. Dean Rusk believed the latter highly likely once the Soviet Airborne Forces had overwhelmed the Israelis. They would retake the Golan Heights and march into Israel itself, a total disaster. President Johnson demanded that the Israelis end their advance into Syria, while he sent the two Sixth Fleet carrier Battle groups nearer to the Syrian coast. The Israeli-Syrian Cease-Fire came not

a moment too soon. As the Duke of Wellington said after the Battle of Waterloo, " It was a very close run thing".

The USS *LIBERTY* was in the middle of knowing more than the Israelis would tolerate. In the heat of battle and crisis nations can make disastrous mistakes. The Israelis made such an unconscionable and monumental error of judgment, quite deliberate and well planned. Moreover, their advance into Syria bought superpower confrontation dangerously close. The timing of the *LIBERTY* attack was such that Washington knew that the Soviet Union was not responsible. Mr. Walsh is to be praised for revealing the glaring errors in the Cristol thesis.

What were the dynamics of communications during this critical period? What may *LIBERTY* have been listening to? In terms of the classified details I hope that the US government under the 40 year rule will release some or all of the material in 2008, though I suspect that the US may follow the British model with some material and wait 50 years. Please note that the UK is a serious player because of the special relationship and sharing of intelligence, particularly communications intelligence. What the UK eventually releases will be revealing, but hold your breath, we may have to wait a long time. The British are still releasing World War Two classified information.

Please remember one simple observation: The US was interested in everyone's communications: Soviet, Israeli, Syrian, Jordanian, Egyptian, and

all their communications with their allies and friends, and in particular the operations of their intelligence services. We could learn a lot from Soviet communications, as much if not more than from Israeli communications. It is like one great game of hearsay. This would be a good time to say that I hope that the new book that is being researched and written regarding *LIBERTY* will include an extensive visit to the Moscow archives in an attempt to get into the Soviet Communications intelligence archives, as well as those of the KGB and the GRU. In addition, the non Soviet Warsaw Pact intelligence agencies' archives are invaluable sources since they will include material that the Russians may not release. There are fluent Russian speakers who may volunteer their time to help unravel the material.

What does Tony Wells think about the specifics of the Israeli attack? Like Dean Rusk I have no doubts whatsoever that the Israelis wanted *LIBERTY* sunk without trace and with no survivors, no one to tell what had happened and by whom. The attack was conducted in such a way to minimize communications from *LIBERTY*. I believe that Israel wanted the identity of the attackers to be associated elsewhere, possibly with Egypt. I am not a conspiracy theory advocate. I deal in hard facts. *LIBERTY*'s destruction ensured that she could no longer collect vital intelligence, while potentially garnering US support through a false belief that one of the Arab world countries had been responsible. Perhaps it might even push the US over the edge, or at least leave it totally neutral interna-

tionally about Israel's invasion of Syria, and possible entry into the outskirts of Damascus, while privately supporting Israel. However, a retaliatory strike by the US against, for example, Egyptian airfields would have precipitated the very crisis that Dean Rusk sought to avert. If the Israelis had continued into Syria and we had attacked Egyptian airfields, we can only speculate on the consequences for Soviet actions. The Israelis could have dragged the US into a war without us really knowing why. I believe that Israel had no concern for the consequences of its actions for US-Soviet relations, as long as Israel's security objectives were achieved. These objectives would be achieved by any means and at any cost. I firmly believe that this summarizes the philosophy behind Israel's planning and execution of the Six Day War. *LIBERTY*'s survival denied Israel the ability to exploit its loss, and thus compelled President Johnson to urge restraint on Israel's advances, together with intense pressure from Moscow. The brave crew of the *LIBERTY* ensured that the ship survived. They fought their ship with all means at their disposal. This fact of courage and survival is the enduring hallmark and legacy of the USS *LIBERTY*. To paraphrase Winston Churchill, They did not give up and they did not surrender.

What else can we all do as a group? Several things I believe. Admiral Merlin Staring has written an incredibly erudite and accurate Statement that was presented to the Senate Armed Services Committee and to the Secretary of Defense. As a vehicle for political action I think that we all know that it will

not generate action, and for reasons that I need not articulate. However, that document is vital in my opinion for the record and for ensuring that later generations understand what happened, and that indeed *LIBERTY*'s crew were victims of egregious war crimes. Publication of Merlin's Statement is critical. As the JAG who investigated in 1967, and as the subsequent Chief Naval Judge Advocate when Senator Warner was Secretary of the Navy, Merlin's Statement has enormous credibility and will hold extraordinary respect with any open minded researcher and historian. In addition, the new book that is to be written should be thorough and meticulous and get into all the issues in fine detail. At some point the media will cease to be controlled regarding USS *LIBERTY.* Those who are not controlled and believe that the truth must be told will prevail. It is the American way. It will take time, but it will happen. The only caution I make is avoid any form of sensationalism at all cost. For examples, pursuing what the CIA wild card James Jesus Angleton got up to, and what our submarines were doing are factors, but they will not change very much, just send the public down wild, sensationalized goose chases. Not a good idea. Having the support of the right media channels is critical – open, honest, professional – that is what we need. They are out there. Let's go find them and take the cause of the *LIBERTY* to them.

I would like to conclude with two points: The long term resolution of the Israeli-Palestinian crisis depends on the US being a true honest broker and working with the international community in

reducing the current boundaries to something near to the pre 1967 June War boundaries, while making some boundary concessions to Israel in order to guarantee its long term security and survivability.

My last point is that the brave men of the *LIBERTY*, by fighting for their ship and not giving up, saved the United States from a potentially disastrous embroilment with the Soviet Union over Israel. Therefore, the US Navy should always have a major Fleet unit Named *LIBERTY*, permanently commemorating the heroism of its brave crew.

Thank you again for giving me this opportunity to be with you all and to do my small piece to honor you all and those brave shipmates who are not with us. Your spirit and courage will endure forever. This is your legacy.

Chapter 10

Conclusion

Cause & Effect

Once again, the "cause" of the sharp turn in America's Middle East foreign policy was the Johnson Administration's unconditional **blind** support for Israel with subsequent congressional support. I believe it was to gain domestic political leverage with the Jewish voters as they were against the Viet Nam War. His efforts paid off as they supported him for re-election. In addition, the military industrial complex lobby prospered with massive military equipment sales to Israel.

Prior Warnings

Military Industrial lobby

On Jan. 17, 1961, President Dwight Eisenhower gave the nation a dire warning about what he described as a threat to democratic government. He called it the "military-industrial complex"—a formidable union of defense contractors and the armed forces. He stated, "In the councils of government, we must guard against the acquisition of unwarranted influence, whether sought or unsought, by the military-industrial complex. The potential for the disastrous rise of misplaced power exists, and will persist."

Foreign Entanglements

Are you aware of President George Washington's warning to avoid foreign entanglements in his farewell speech? Washington goes on to urge the American people to take advantage of their isolated position in the world, and avoid attachments and entanglements in foreign affairs, especially those of Europe, which he argues have little or nothing to do with the interests of America. He argues that it makes no sense for the American people to wage war on European soil when their isolated position and unity will allow them to remain neutral and focus on their own affairs. As a result, Washington argues that the country should avoid permanent alliance with **all** foreign nations, although temporary alliances during times of extreme danger may be necessary.

Both Thomas Jefferson was worried about "entangling alliances" and John Quincy Adam gave a speech on July 4, 1821 indicating it was neither America's duty nor its destiny to go "abroad in search of monsters to destroy."

Congress indirectly Supports Apartheid

Former President Jimmy Carter's book entitled, "Palestine, Peace not Apartheid" clearly identifies Israel creating a Palestinian structure that mirrors the previous South African government (before its white controlled apartheid was dismantled and its black and white citizens were allowed to form a representative government). Carter's reason for writing his book was to jar Congressmen and the American public to begin debate as to the current situation in Palestine.

The Israeli government is creating the same apartheid structure. In other words, do we want to be a party to this same suppressive situation in Palestine? Can't we see that we are losing our sense of values? Do the Israeli supporters have that much control over our Congress? Instead of appreciating Carter's words of wisdom and instead of taking an objective approach to Carter's details, he was immediately labeled "anti-Semitic" even from is own party.

Note: As with former President Carter's book, if this book brings a fair and objective debate that would be wonderful.

The Effect

While there were some Congressmen who initially protested, they soon realized they were being labeled "anti-Semitic". This blind support for Israel resulted in the *Liberty* crew suffering the bigotry cited in the aforementioned chapters because we demanded the truth be told. It is not my attempt to damn Israel or Jews but to raise a flag of awareness to the fact our country has lost its way and lost its values. We have been coerced and made to feel Holocaust guilt for not supporting Israel by **American** Israeli supporters. The military industrial complex lobby is also implicated. How do we rid ourselves from this dilemma?

Our ordeal exemplifies a dark side about our politicians and our political system. That is, our politicians should put Americans first over any foreign government especially one whose military would attempt to murder 294 Americans in 1967 (USS *Liberty*) and spit and curse American

Marines in 1982 in Lebanon (cited in the book "Cursed is the Peacemaker" by John Boykin). The IDF murdered thirty-four of my shipmates which included one NSA civilian, two marines, and thirty-one sailors. In addition to the loss of American lives, the Israelis destroyed one of the most advanced intelligence ships of the day. I am also aware Israel murdered Americans Rachel Corrie and Furkan Dogan. Both Republican and Democratic chief executives and subsequent Congresses have done nothing. How many more Americans must be slaughtered by Israel before our government responds accordingly?

As indicated in Patrick Buchanan's book, "A Republic Not An Empire," America has provided Israel $100 billion over the years. Israel is the twenty-second richest country in the world. This is absurd. Israel takes whatever territory is wants in the West Bank and disregards complaints from the U.S. They even sell advanced weapons dependent on U.S. technology to China.

The USS *Liberty* story is a microcosm to a much bigger issue as to what changed in 1967. The failure to investigate rests squarely on the people's house, the House of Representatives. The change must be studied, discussed, and debated in the halls of Congress. In order for this to happen, Congress must investigate the attack as required by our Constitution. When the *Liberty* crew is requested to provide testimony under oath, I am confident that the result would indicate the attack was deliberate. I would also hope the details are released to the public once a federal investigation has been completed. That would be a turning point

in our nation's evolvement to a higher state and a return to our values.

What is Congress Thinking?

Why are Congress and the Pentagon so against an honest *Liberty* investigation? After all, they say it was an accidental attack. If that were true, the investigation would permanently silence us. And since they are so sure it was accidental, they would have nothing to loose.

The only conclusion the *Liberty* crew can deduce is that the order to sink the ship came from a very high Israeli government source the US wants to protect, or the US was also involved, and/or Johnson violated the law. Since 1967, there has been something very diabolical about the US-Israeli relationship. From everything I have read, many Americans feel the same way but are not sure what exactly is the cause for their suspicious feelings. The fabrications the news media documents are another reason people are suspicious because other news sources provide different outcomes.

Could the problem be Israeli supporters, Congressional and news media control?

Please analyze the following scenario. How much evidence do you need to be convinced?

American spy Jonathon Pollard, who spied for Israel, did massive damage to our intelligence network. The

damage to our intelligence network was severe but yet, some Congressmen want our President to pardon this traitor. Israel has been pleading for his release for years and has indicated Mr. Pollard has an Israeli villa waiting for him. Pollard's damage was terrible, but Israel's actions were even worse. That is, the Mossad (Israel's CIA) traded military secrets which included names, hardware, and fighter aircraft specifications to the Soviets for the release of Russian Jews to immigrate to Israel. The result placed our friendly foreign spies' life in mortal jeopardy and shut down the intelligence reporting on secret Russian activity. Our close so called Middle East friend and ally should have protected our intelligence network; however, instead, they used the information as a bargaining chip with the Soviets and other hostile countries for their own personal gain. The bottom line is Israel has its own interests and the Pollard travesty proves they would stab us in the back if they benefit. The following is a list of Congressmen supporting Pollard's release: Barney Frank (retired), Gary L. Ackerman, Robert F. Andrews, Shelley Berkley, Robert A. Brady, Danny Davis, Theodore E. Deutsch, Eliot L. Engel, John J. Hall, James A. Himes, Maurice D. Hinchey, Sheila Jackson Lee, Patrick J. Kennedy, John Lewis, Carolyn B. Maloney, Michael E. McMahon, Gregory W. Meeks, Jerrod Nadler, Eleanor Holmes Norton, John W. Olver, Frank Pallone, Jr., Bill Pascrell, Jr., Donald M. Payne, Charles B. Rangel, Laura Richardson, Janice D. Schakowsky, Robert C. Scott, Brad Sherman, Bennie G. Thompson, Edolphus Towns, Nikki Tsongas, Henry A. Waxman, and Anthony Weiner (resigned).

These Congressmen have indicated they put Israel before American interests. Are your Congressmen on the above list? Has your Senator or Representative visited Israel recently? If and when the media reports same, write it down. I am not saying they should never visit Israel; however, the frequency of the visits is important. If they vote routinely to support, defend Israel despite belligerent behavior, and they visit Israel frequently – **they should be voted out as quickly as possible.**

Intention

I am not saying we should turn our backs on Israel, however, Congress should demand the name or names of those who ordered the Liberty attack. If that person or persons are still alive, they should be taken to task if Israel wants to remain our close friend. Congress should also debate our relationship. That is, what does Congress do to tame the 800 pound Gorilla in the room —a belligerent Israel? I hope by now, you understand and agree the U.S. government has contributed to this situation. Our fundamental action must be to develop a balanced and objective Middle East foreign policy. This would include condemning Israel, when appropriate, for breaking international law at the United Nations, the Geneva Convention, and the World Court in The Hague. Additionally, Israel is the twenty- second richest country in the world and the United States must stand down from supplying her with arms and money. Thirdly, Israel will remain belligerent if we indicate Israel's' security is our security. She must stand on her own hopefully making peace with her neighbors the hard way – negotiations and compromise.

Note: I wonder if any Congressmen know Israel machine gunned our life rafts making them un-useable if we had to abandon ship. In any case, we should not assign a single American service man or woman on Israeli soil. My discussions with current Navy personnel is that they are leaving the Navy rather than be put in a situation to fight for Israel or experience long deployments and separation from their families in order to support Israel.

However, to put things in perspective, I am not naïve about fanatical Islamics. From everything I have read and deduced, the Islamic religion is very self centered and suppressive. When you add Sharia Law, effected populace will not grow mentally beyond the fifteenth century. The Islamics will not rest until they have complete control over all people and real estate they occupy. They are not dumb either and their scientists will attempt to match our military mite as much as possible. The west can contain this militancy the same way we contained the Soviet Union. Fighting amongst themselves is their problem not ours. America should not use military intervention; however, if and when an Islamic nation belligerently attacks a non-Islamic country, if asked, America should respond militarily only if a quick and decisive effort is forecast. In other words as with the Soviets the operative word was "containment". In order to stay out of their wars, America must be totally oil independent without any thirst for their oil whatsoever. The fanatical Islamcis will never give up. Overwhelming military strength is the only thing they understand.

America cannot and should not attempt to prevent the

cruelty of Sharia Law within an Islamic country. If the populace rejects it, we should not attempt to provide military intervention. That would be an internal matter for their people to resolve. America does not and should not have any military based within Islamic territory. History indicates no country has gotten their way in another country's civil war. Does Vietnam ring a bell? The Islamic struggle is theirs, not ours unless they go beyond their borders.

The Islamics have stated their desire to see all western troops removed from their territory. Why not accommodate them? We do not need to have our servicemen and women available to be **local targets.** Should any Islamic country be too dangerous for our diplomatic corps, we should leave the country unless the host country can guarantee our safety. There is no need to place our service and diplomatic core in harm's way. In time, by returning to our core values, we will become united internally and develop international friends that want to do business with us, especially moderate Islamics. Only Congress can effectively turn this around.

A balanced Middle East Foreign Policy may influence the more moderate Islamic countries to cooperate with the United States and our allies as it did during the fifties and sixties. The point is the current level of violence may cease or be curtailed once America is observed being equally fair to both Arabs and Israelis.

Without our blind support and financial assistance, Israel would hopefully accommodate its neighbors and develop compassion for the displaced Palestinians. They

would not have a country if it were not for Palestinian land. Hopefully, they would come to understand the grief everyone has suffered since 1948 and make the best of it for all. Can't our Congress understand that Palestinians have suffered long enough?

The *Liberty* story is the clearest and strongest example of our disastrous blind support for Israel which has resulted in all the evils our founding fathers have warned us about. Once Congress completes an objective *Liberty* investigation, as stated, I believe America will divorce itself from supporting a belligerent and tyrannical ally. I do not believe we should become "isolationist" – I would hope we would get our military completely out of the Middle East. As far as the rest of the world, we should stay out of other people's affairs. Nevertheless, America should "walk softly and carry a very big visible stick". So as not to repeat past mistakes, our intelligence organizations should be maintained and continue to be the "trip wire" to protect our country.

Serving Our Country

Let me quote the military oath and please pay attention to these words carefully. "I solemnly swear and affirm that I will support and defend the Constitution of the United States against all enemies, foreign or domestic; that I will bear true faith and allegiance to the same; and I will obey the orders of the President of the United States and the orders of the officers appointed over me, according to regulations and the Uniform Code of Military Justice. So help me God."

In addition, let me also point out that under the Uniform Code of Military Justice, Article 99 entitled, "Misbehavior before the enemy," sub-paragraph 9: "Any person who does not afford all practicable relief and assistance to any troops, combatants, vessels, or aircraft of the armed forces belonging to the United States or their allies when engaged in battle shall be punished by death or such punishment as a court-martial may direct." Shouldn't the President or the Secretary of Defense be held to the same standard as someone in uniform? Was that one of the reasons the '67 Navy Court of Inquiry was falsified? If Congress investigated and came to that same conclusion, would that mean they would have to charge and impeach President Johnson?

By placing our country back on a more peaceful track, the above should be taken into consideration for future Chief Executives. Only Congress has the power to place the appropriate controls.

As time passes, it will become increasingly more difficult for the US Government and the IDF to maintain their cover up and lie because it has become apparent to the crew of the USS Liberty, more and more people believe we are telling the truth. Also, more and more prominent Americans will be speaking out on our behalf. Time is on our side because the longer we or possibly our children speak out and are recognized by the occasional objective reporter, the number of years we have struggled will make avoiding the truth increasingly more difficult to maintain. In other words—why would these veteran sailors become activist and dig their heels in for so many years? Why? For the Truth! I believe in the CIA's motto, "Truth will set you free".

More and more Americans and Europeans as well as some Israelis are anxious to see peace in the Middle East and also realize the current Israeli belligerency is not the answer.

The Answer lies with Congress

Americans must become aware of this internal and external threat. Don't you think Congress should be curious and anxious about the Israeli attack? No, instead they are hiding behind their desks. The *Liberty* crew and many others have tried to get their attention. I personally have requested help many times without any results. I maintain Congress, operating as the representative body of ALL Americans, is the tool to place America back on the fair and balance approach to all international issues.

Americans need to take back the halls of Congress—your choice folks! The following is so vitally important. The current Congressional situation is this: it is more important to fund, protect, and defend Israel over and above our own citizens and military. The USS *Liberty* is the prime example of this. Please stand up for the thirty-four crewmen of the USS *Liberty* who were killed in hostile action, their grieving families, and the USS *Liberty* crew who are still alive. The Navy lost one of its prime intelligence ships. Please remember the USS *Liberty* is the most decorated US Navy ship for a single engagement. This situation must change. I hope you realize our success through Congress is also America's success as it would indicate Congress is free of Israeli control.

In addition, I never want to see our military or our citizenry attacked by the IDF ever again. If any of you have a family member or friend in the active military or diplomatic service, let me give you some advice. If they are co-located with the IDF please advise them to watch their backs and do whatever is necessary to stay safe, as the IDF will do whatever **they** feel is necessary to prosper in a situation even if you are in their way. How can I make such a statement? So far, **History** indicates Congressmen will **not** come to their aid or support but will side with Israel. Since history repeats itself, and the IDF was never held accountable for killing our military because of our government's inabilities to take them to task; then logically, our current servicemen are at risk. **Never Again! Please Never Again!** Based on what happened to us, my fear is it could happen again and Admiral Mullen, former Chairman of the Joint Chiefs, agrees.

The Usefulness of Prayer

Please understand that I have my faults as well as everyone else. But, I would like to pass this concept along as it opened my eyes. As an altar boy growing up in Philadelphia in the fifties, there was a prayer said in English at the bottom of the alter stairs at the very end of the Latin Mass. The priest said, "Mary, holy mother of God, save Russia". As I remember, this prayer was said for years. Who would have ever contemplated that Russia as mighty militarily as it was with an atheistic communist government and extremely powerful, would have collapsed in a matter of weeks? And it happened without a fighting war! As massive and powerful

as it was, I believe prayer and a higher power played a role. As a result, I understand the Russian Orthodox Church has rebounded and is flourishing today. What do our clergy have to lose if they all said a prayer at the end of their respective service asking for God's help to restore peace, harmony, and equality for everyone in Palestine? Or, "Lord, please give our Congress the grace to be fair and respectful to all peoples and religions". Why is that so wrong? Why aren't they doing it on their own? Are they concerned this prayer would be offensive to some of their listeners? Think about it. Catholic Bishops, what about you? It worked before.

I have one more point to make about religion. I have been told ninety percent of Christians have fled the Holy Land since Israel became its master in 1967. Why are they leaving? Because of their lack of parishioners, the churches there are in financial trouble. One of the reasons is the Israeli settlers are belligerent and hostile to Christian priests. An eastern rite Catholic Church canonized one of their priests a few years ago because he was killed for refusing to take down external crucifixes adorning his Church as they found them offensive. The situation is not appropriate to discuss in my book, however, I leave you with that thought and hope you do your own research. Is our news media deliberately not reporting negative Israeli events?

Please get fired up and concerned. Tell your family, friends, and neighbors about these details. If you cannot or will not believe me, please do your own research as it is too important to just walk away from this problem.

I pray you do this for our future and our grand children's future. May God continue to bless America!

Note: I have a confession to make. I have sinned. I have broken the Eleventh Commandment. "Thou shall not criticize Israel or her supporters".

If I am wrong or naïve, our troops will NEVER stop fighting wars in the Middle East or North Africa. Our homeland will always be at risk from Fanatical Islamics. I hope our Congress will eventually understand and appreciate this thought. It all begins with an honest and objective congressional investigation of the USS *Liberty* attack. May the thirty-four *Liberty* crew killed in the attack not have died in vein? Amen.

message, you will complete this book with a fire in your stomach and become a *Liberty* and American activist—that is, tell your family and friends and write the president, your senators and representatives.

Note: I created the first chapter to hopefully "prime the pump" to peak your interest and ignite your American spirit.

> Webster's New World Dictionary (Third College Edition) defines BIGOT as a person who holds blindly and intolerantly to a particular creed, opinion, etc.

label. Others of the same bias in power positions will not tolerate any negativity toward Israel.

The above did not happen overnight. I have witnessed the change starting in 1967 and this is what I hope you will learn and understand in my book. If you do not agree with me, it is your right but I hope you have sound justification to maintain your skepticism. The events are true and as accurate as I can remember. Since Congress did not investigate the attack and as you will discover, the Navy Court of Inquiry was a sham, there are currently unknowns as circumstances and details of the USS *Liberty* still remain classified. After over forty-five years, one has to wonder why?

My motivation to write this book comes from my love of country—not to tear it down—but to see the necessary dialogue return to Congress. We must deal with reality and truth before we take steps to correct the problem—then and only then will we be able to see a fair and balanced Middle East foreign policy as it was prior to 1967. I hope to see American values return to our society. I pray there will come a time when the Jewish-American War Veterans and other Jewish organizations will invite me to speak at one of their meetings and actually listen to my presentation. They do not have to agree—just refrain from harassment and anti-Semitic labeling. My experience with the Jewish-American War Veterans at this time is that they will not tolerate Israeli criticism.

The USS *Liberty* story is vitally important to American citizens on many different levels. If you appreciate my

Prologue

I grew up in a little Italy in northern Philadelphia in a warm and loving family. My sister, Lorraine, and I are third generation Italian-Americans. We attended St. Mary's of the Eternal Church which provided "K" through eight grades. Our first rate teachers were mostly nuns of the Franciscan order with a few lay teachers. I received twelve years of great parochial school. The point I wish to make is the sound and secure American value foundation I obtained from role models, priests, nuns, scouting, parents, and a great education. In my twenties with the maturity for greater appreciation, the more I studied American history, the more love of country grew.

The events over the years regarding the Middle East and the bigotry I experienced have greatly troubled me. Yes, America, we have a major problem because of our blind support for Israel. The checks and balances of Congress have failed us miserably. Enhanced with a lack of criticism coming from our legislative body for Israeli actions, a bias develops. Therefore, the Israeli supporters gain strength and their personal labels on individuals and organization that cross them takes on a sense of accuracy to include "anti-Semitic." In other words, when Israeli critics identify inappropriate Israeli or Israeli supporter's actions, the lack of criticism from our politicians enhance the anti-Semitic

Contents

Dedication

This book is dedicated to the thirty-four USS *Liberty* crew, the *Liberty* crew who have since died, and all Navy sailors, marines, and NSA civilians who have paid the ultimate price. They are American heroes and have not been forgotten and will some day reach America's place of honor.

I also dedicate this book to my wife, Patricia, who has supported me and all that it entails to expose the USS Liberty truth.

Liberty Injustices:
A Survivor's Account of American Bigotry

Copyright © 2013 by Ernest A. Gallo

This book is the account of the author's survival of the attack on the USS Liberty and the events that have followed the incident.

Cover Design by Geared Graphics.
All rights reserved.
Contributed Artwork by Lars Underbakke
All rights reserved.
Interior Book Layout by Kathleen M Shea

ISBN 978-1-935795-20-9 (hc)
ISBN 978-1-935795-19-3 (sc)
LCCN 2013946490

ClearView Press, Inc.
PO Box 353431
Palm Coast, FL 32135-3431
www.clearviewpressinc.com

Printed in the United States of America

Liberty Injustices
A Survivor's Account of American Bigotry

By

Ernest A. Gallo

ClearView Press, Inc.
Palm Coast, FL

Liberty Injustices